HALDANE OF CLOAN

Richard Burdon Haldane

DUDLEY SOMMER

HALDANE
OF CLOAN

His Life and Times

1856–1928

Ruskin House

GEORGE ALLEN & UNWIN LTD

MUSEUM STREET LONDON

PRINTED IN GREAT BRITAIN
in 12 on 13 point Bembo type
BY JARROLD AND SONS LIMITED
NORWICH

For
R. M. S.

PREFACE

I have first to express my gratitude to Her Majesty the Queen for her gracious permission to make use of material from the Royal Archives at Windsor. At the same time I would like to acknowledge the kindness I have received from all concerned with the Royal Archives and notably from Sir Owen Morshead, until recently Librarian at Windsor Castle, and also from his successor, Mr Robert Mackworth-Young.

For information concerning the general political and social background of the period covered by Haldane's life I am in debt to many historians and writers. In particular I should like to acknowledge the invaluable assistance I have derived from the late Sir Robert Ensor's *England 1870–1914* (Oxford University Press) and Sir Harold Nicolson's *King George V—His Life and Reign* (Constable). These brilliant studies have been a constant source of information and inspiration and I am glad of this opportunity of acknowledging my indebtedness. Sir Harold Nicolson has moreover increased my debt to him in most generously saving me a great deal of additional research in the Royal Archives at Windsor by allowing me to make use of material from that source which he himself has used in his Life of King George V.

Concerning Haldane himself, my first acknowledgement must be to the late Major-General Sir Frederick Maurice's two-volume Life of Lord Haldane (Faber and Faber). His initial work in sifting the mass of material—letters, memoranda and the like—at the biographer's disposal has lightened my labours in this respect appreciably. Furthermore his special qualifications to assess Haldane's work at the War Office have been of the greatest value in preparing this book. I am grateful to General Maurice's son—Mr F. M. P. Maurice—for permission to quote from these volumes.

I am indebted to the late General Sir Aylmer Haldane's book *The Haldanes of Gleneagles* (Blackwood) for valuable information concerning Lord Haldane's grandfather and great-uncle, which appears in the chapter *Scottish Inheritance*.

When I try to express my appreciation of those who have helped me personally in my task I am at a loss—not where to start but where to end. My first acknowledgement must be to the Haldane family and in particular to Mrs M. E. Campbell Fraser, Mr T. G. N. Haldane, and Mr A. R. B. Haldane. Without their initial permission to use the material now held by the National Library of Scotland this book could not have been written at all. Their deep interest in my work has been evidenced in countless ways—by many introductions to men and women who could contribute something to the Haldane story and by their kindly advice and valuable suggestions at every stage of the journey.

My gratitude extends to many men and women who knew Lord Haldane personally or were specially qualified to speak of some aspect of his life and work. With them I have either talked or corresponded, and in many cases they have gone to the trouble of preparing memoranda to record their assessment of Lord Haldane's work and character or some story or incident connected with him. It is hardly possible to name all who have so generously responded to my enquiries; some are already mentioned specifically in this book but I would like to record my indebtedness to the following in addition:

Lady Aitchison, the late Lord Alness, the late Rt Hon. L. S. Amery, Lord Ammon, Sir Norman Angell, the late Lord Asquith of Bishopstone, Mrs Raymond Asquith, the Duchess of Atholl, the Rt Hon. Harold Baker, Lord Balfour of Burleigh, Sir Ernest Barker, Lord Beaverbrook, Lord and the late Lady Beveridge, Mr Robert Blake, Sir Maurice Bonham Carter, Lady Violet Bonham Carter, Lieut-Colonel J. H. Boraston, Brigadier Sir Alick Buchanan-Smith, the late Mrs Carruthers (Miss Violet Markham), the late Viscount Cecil of Chelwood, Mr W. F. Clarke (for allowing me to use a memorandum prepared by his father, the late Sir Edward Clarke, a passage from which is quoted on page 349), Mrs Costin, Sir Herbert Creedy, Sir William Charles Crocker, the late Dr Winifred Cullis, the late Mr Lionel Curtis, the late Major-General Sir John Davidson, Lord Elibank, Viscount Esher (for permission to quote from his father's book *Journals and Letters of Reginald, Viscount Esher*), Sir Newman Flower, Mr Roger Fulford (for his kind encouragement and advice), Dr G. P. Gooch, Mr John Gore, the late Dr Philip Gosse (who most generously allowed me to quote certain extracts from his father's unpublished Diary), General Sir Hubert Gough, Lord Hankey, Mr Wilfrid Hunt, Lady Iddesleigh, the late Dean Inge, the late Dr L. P. Jacks, the late Dr

Thomas Jones, the late Earl Jowitt, Dr J. F. Lockwood (Master of Birkbeck College), the Rev. Innes Logan, Mr Ian Macnaughton, Mr Joseph Macleod, Lord McNair, the late Viscount Mersey, the late Viscountess Milner, the late Professor J. H. Morgan, Mr W. G. Morris, the Rt Hon. Herbert Morrison, Mr Hector Munro (who kindly undertook the laborious task of copying out many pages from his grandfather's [Lieut-General Sir Spencer Ewart] Diary referring to Haldane), the late Dr Gilbert Murray, the Hon. Sir Albert Napier, the late Viscount Norwich, the late Sir Robert Overbury, the late Baron Palmstierna, Lady Pentland, Lord Pethick-Lawrence, the late Lord Quickswood, Sir Sarvepalli Radhakrishnan, Earl Russell (Bertrand Russell), the late Mr Geoffrey Russell, Mr A. P. Ryan, Lord Salter, Lord Samuel, the late Miss Sankey, Mr L. O. Sharp, the late Viscount Simon, Sir Henry Slesser, the late Mr Wickham Steed, Sir Campbell Stuart, Professor R. H. Tawney, Professor Arnold Toynbee, the late Marshal of the Royal Air Force Viscount Trenchard, the late Sir Charles Trevelyan, Dr G. M. Trevelyan, the late Professor Clement C. J. Webb, Sir Frederick Whyte, and Mr James Young.

I would like to acknowledge the unfailing kindness I have received from the National Library of Scotland, whose patience has been inexhaustible. I acknowledge, too, my indebtedness to the Brotherton Library of Leeds University, who hold the Haldane-Gosse correspondence, not only for their permission to use this material but for their kind assistance on numerous occasions.

I have to acknowledge with thanks permission to quote from L. S. Amery's *My Political Life* (Hutchinson); J. K. Dunlop's *The Development of the British Army 1899–1914* (Methuen); R. C. K. Ensor's *England 1870–1914* (Oxford University Press); *Journals and Letters of Reginald, Viscount Esher* (Ivor Nicholson & Watson); Carl J. Friedrich's *The Philosophy of Hegel* (Random House Inc.); Haldane's *Autobiography* (Hodder & Stoughton); Philip Magnus's *Kitchener* (John Murray); Harold Nicolson's *King George V—His Life and Reign* (Constable); Bertrand Russell's *A History of Western Philosophy* (Allen & Unwin); J. A. Spender's and Cyril Asquith's *Life of Herbert Henry Asquith, Lord Oxford and Asquith* (Hutchinson); and G. M. Trevelyan's *Grey of Fallodon* (Longmans).

If by ill chance I have failed either here or in the text to make proper acknowledgement of material used, I crave the indulgence of those concerned and ask them to accept my sincere apologies.

I would like to express my appreciation of the great kindness I have received from the Rt Hon. Sir Norman Brook (Secretary of the Cabinet) whenever I have sought his guidance or help.

I am most grateful to my friend the Dean of St Paul's (the Very Reverend W. R. Matthews) for kindly reading in proof the chapter on 'Philosophy' and for his encouragement throughout the years I have spent in preparing this volume.

I had the great good fortune when this book was in typescript to meet Mr Gordon Carey, who has not only been kind enough to read the whole book both in manuscript and in proof, but has also undertaken the exacting task of compiling the index. This he has accomplished with outstanding success. I might add that, with his expert knowledge of book production, his suggestions have been invaluable in countless other ways.

My final acknowledgement is to Mrs Hilda Cannings, who typed the book—many chapters many times! She never evinced any sign of the weariness she must so often have felt; on the contrary her enthusiasm was contagious and I am deeply grateful.

SPRING POND, MIDHURST

January 1960

D. S.

CONTENTS

ILLUSTRATIONS

The just man and firm of purpose
not the heat of fellow citizens
clamouring for what is wrong, nor
presence of threatening tyrant can
shake in his rocklike soul.

HORACE: *Odes*

Truth is the cry of all, but the
game of few. Certainly, where it
is the chief passion, it doth not
give way to vulgar cares and views,
nor is it contented with a little
ardour in the early time of life;
active perhaps to pursue, but not
so fit to weigh and revise. He who
would make a real progress in knowledge
must dedicate his age as well as
youth, the later growth as well as
first fruits, at the altar of Truth.

Bishop GEORGE BERKELEY: *Siris*

The Wise
Have still the keeping of their proper peace,
Are guardians of their own tranquillity.

WORDSWORTH: *The Excursion*

PROLOGUE

In the constantly moving story of human endeavour and experience there occur, or appear to occur, periods when the pace of change is accelerated—when, during a comparatively short space of time, events of deep significance arise. The seventy-two years of Haldane's life (1856–1928) would seem to cover such a period.

Queen Victoria was thirty-seven years of age when Richard Burdon Haldane was born in 1856 and was to reign for a further forty-five years. Palmerston had formed his first Cabinet in 1855, but such was the political confusion between 1846 (following the break-up of the Conservative Party) and the passing of the Reform Bill of 1867 that there were no fewer than nine Administrations in twenty-one years. Sir Llewellyn Woodward,[1] commenting on the political insecurity of those days, points out that the very names of the Parties were unstable for a time. The Queen had little liking for the shrewd, worldly, and often flippant Palmerston, and on his appointment she wrote in her Journal ' . . . not personally agreeable to me but I think of nothing but the country'.

This was certainly true in this instance and the credit can be shared equally between the Queen and her Prime Minister. She always found it hard, however, to be fair, let alone generous, to this man, who when he died at the age of eighty-one had been a Minister of the Crown, with short intervals, for fifty-eight years. Palmerston was a man of very great gifts who enjoyed conducting the country's foreign affairs as a poker player—the more perilous the cards he held, the better he liked it—and so often he was right!

The Queen had developed greatly, under the tuition of the Prince Consort, since the days of 'good Lord Melbourne', who was still remembered with affection. There were signs, however, that a new star of great brilliance had appeared in the heavens in the person of Benjamin Disraeli, who ultimately captured the Queen's admiration and affection as no other Prime Minister during her long reign. Lord

[1] E. L. Woodward, *The Age of Reform 1815–1870* (O.U.P.)

Melbourne was the friend and counsellor of her youth, in whom she reposed infinite trust. Disraeli was to become the confidant and guide of her maturity. In 1856, however, her confidence and affection rested only in her beloved Albert; the years of happiness had not yet run their course.

The 'right' to govern still belonged to the privileged classes in 1856 and few working men had votes. The idea that some of these men might one day find their way into the House of Commons was met by the argument (expressed in the debates on the Reform Bill in 1860) that they would waste time in discussions upon wages and the relation between capital and labour and other matters 'which did not lie within the province of legislation'.

It was in Palmerston's second and last Administration, formed in 1859, that Gladstone secured the succession to the leadership of the Liberal Party after Palmerston and Russell.

The political scene during Haldane's youth and early manhood was dominated by the figures of Gladstone and Disraeli. The duel between these two has no counterpart in English history, except perhaps the rivalry of Pitt and Fox. Neither was in the main stream of political leadership, for neither was an aristocrat by birth: Gladstone (whilst educated at Eton and Oxford) came from the mercantile class; Disraeli was a baptised Jew. The Queen's antipathy to Gladstone and her affection and admiration for Disraeli never fail to intrigue historians and biographers, which is understandable.

Gladstone's mind was engrossed with theology and morals in their widest application. His power of exposition was unrivalled and he gave voice to the beliefs and aspirations of a large section of the middle class. For them the 'live coals from off the altar' had touched his lips. In a world slowly moving from privilege to democracy Gladstone was a superb leader. With his passionate desire to seek a better world, to see wrongs righted and improvements made, went a fundamental respect for antiquity. He did not desire change for its own sake but only if it could be shown as an alternative to injustice or gave promise of that better world for which he so earnestly strove. If this be true, what then was there in this man which repelled so many, and notably the Queen? Perhaps Gladstone's intellect was over-subtle and tortuous, so that in his anxiety to achieve what he believed to be desirable ends he used means which were less desirable. But all the criticisms of him cannot destroy the picture of a great and extraordinary man—his amazing intellect, his passionate hatred of cruelty and oppression, his oratory, his political sagacity, the simplicity of his private life, and the depth of his religious faith were a combination seldom if ever seen in such strength before or since.

The romantic, elusive figure of Benjamin Disraeli is difficult to capture. He was a man of great imaginative insight. Algernon Cecil in his book *Victoria and her Prime Ministers* says of Disraeli that 'he seemed to know by a kind of racial instinct where to believe and where to doubt'. This instinct was inherent in all his actions and relationships, and because of it he was admired and even loved but never understood. He became the leader of the Conservative Party under the banner of the Monarchy and the Empire. His devotion to both has never been surpassed.

In the autumn of 1860, English eyes were turned towards America. It was evident on the election of Lincoln as President that the long dispute between North and South over the question of slavery was reaching a crisis. The Southern State of North Carolina decided to leave the Union; other States followed and Jefferson Davis was elected President of a new Confederacy. The Northern States refused to recognise the right of secession and in April 1861 the war began. It ended with victory for the Northern forces on 26 May 1865, the British Government having wisely refrained from intervention or mediation.

At home the death of the Prince Consort on 14 December 1861 was an event of far-reaching significance. We have long come to recognise that the Prince was a great man in both character and ability. At the age of forty-two he had already made an indelible mark on many facets of our national life. It is interesting to speculate on the part he would have played in the affairs of his adopted country had he not been cut off in the prime of life. For the Queen the loss was irreparable. To her uncle (the King of the Belgians) she wrote:[1]

Oh! To be cut off in the prime of life—to see our pure, happy, quiet, domestic life which *alone* enabled me to bear my *much* disliked position, CUT OFF at forty-two—when I *had* hoped with such instinctive certainty that God *never* would part us and would let us grow old together (though he always talked of the shortness of life) is *too awful*.

There followed for her the long years of seclusion and loneliness—in large measure self-imposed—when she lost touch, not with affairs of

[1] *The Letters of Queen Victoria* (John Murray).

State but with her people. Gradually, however, she emerged from the shadows and during the last twenty years of her life she came to symbolise the greatness of her Empire.

The year 1867 saw the passing of the Reform Bill, a measure long overdue. It is interesting to note that in 1865, on the death of Palmerston, the adult male population of England and Wales was over five millions, of whom under one million had votes! The Act of 1867 added 938,000 votes to an electorate of 1,056,000. In 1872 the ballot was introduced. Twenty years earlier Palmerston had told his constituents at Tiverton that 'to go sneaking to the ballot-box and poking in a piece of paper is unconstitutional and unworthy of the character of straightforward and honest Englishmen'.[1] Time marches on!

It is necessary to retrace our steps to the year 1862, when an event took place which was to have far-reaching effects on the course of history. Bismarck, then forty-seven, and with no very remarkable career to date, was appointed Minister-President of Prussia. Until his dismissal in 1890 this man of 'blood and iron', built on monumental scale, was to be the virtual ruler of Prussia and ultimately of a united Germany. In place of constitutional government he imposed a dictatorship (in fact if not in name), and when in 1870 Bismarck by adroit design led France into declaring war on Prussia, the political ascendancy over Europe passed from France to Germany. This ascendancy was to continue for forty-four years, in the last ten years of which Haldane, whilst hoping and working for what might today be called 'peaceful co-existence', prepared his country for war.

The conquest of France, completed in six months, was evidence of war's dreadful possibilities as an instrument of policy—it was to usher in what Sir R. C. K. Ensor has so aptly described as 'Europe's long vigil under arms'.[2] How did this event affect the English mind and England's future policy? Never before had a war been so freely reported in the press, and in its short duration the people of this country were to follow the sensational events which led to the siege and fall of Paris. Nor was this all, for public and professional opinion was aroused to the danger, never before considered, of a German invasion of these islands. It was fortunate indeed that the then Secretary for War was a man of vision, courage, and efficiency. Edward Cardwell held office from 1868 until 1874 and his achievements in those few years entitle him to rank as the greatest British War Minister during the nineteenth century. Cardwell

[1] R. C. K. Ensor, *England 1870–1914* (O.U.P.)   [2] *Ibid.*

wanted not only a bigger Army but a reformed Army. He had a long and hard fight. At the top the Commander-in-Chief, the Duke of Cambridge, opposed all change on principle. He was supported on the one hand by the vested interests who wanted only to maintain the *status quo*, and on the other by those who cared for little but a screwing down of the Estimates. What Cardwell did for the British Army in his day will be of peculiar interest to us as we follow the work accomplished by his great successor over thirty years later.

Cardwell started in 1868 by abolishing flogging during peace-time. This was a courageous step to take, for it drew the opposition of most senior officers. He realised, however, that if the private soldier's career was to have any dignity, the Army had got to treat him as a human being and the abuse of power and privilege had got to be eradicated. Two years later he abolished 'bounty money' for recruits and at the same time commenced to discharge known bad characters from the Army. In 1869 he started the withdrawal of troops from the self-governing colonies, thereby encouraging these colonies to raise their own local forces. At the same time it made possible the intensive training of a British Army in this country.

In 1870 the Commander-in-Chief was subordinated to the Secretary of State. Although the Queen reluctantly accepted this principle and signed the Order in Council, she continued for many years to look upon the Army as in some special way belonging to her and she maintained her cousin, the Duke of Cambridge, as Commander-in-Chief until 1895 against great opposition.

In 1871 Cardwell's Army Regulation Bill was introduced into the Commons. It contained one highly contentious feature: it abolished 'purchase'. This was the system whereby rich young men could buy themselves into positions to which many were totally unsuited. Opposition to the abolition of purchase was strong—this was still the age of privilege—but after a fierce struggle it was passed by the Commons, only to be shelved by the Lords, which was tantamount to its rejection. Cardwell, however, finding the direct assault had failed, won his objective by an out-flanking movement: he secured the abolition of purchase by Royal Warrant. When this was announced the Opposition were shrill in condemnation of what they deemed to be an abuse of the Prerogative. It was certainly unusual to seek the Sovereign's aid in this way, but there was nothing illegal or unconstitutional in so doing. The country, however, were behind this energetic and courageous War

Minister; they wanted security and that entailed a stronger and better Army. Furthermore, the Lords found themselves in this predicament: the Bill provided for generous compensation for the officers and unless it was passed there would be none at all. The Lords, therefore, greatly protesting, had perforce to pass the Bill which they had shelved. The abolition of purchase was a considerable victory for Cardwell and the small band of enlightened officers who supported him. In the main the officer class was against him but he was able to rally the Liberals (and notably Gladstone) on the anti-privilege argument.

But for Cardwell this was only a good beginning. He next divided the War Department into three sections, all responsible to the Secretary of State. They were the Commander-in-Chief, the Surveyor-General of the Ordnance, and the Financial Secretary. The Commander-in-Chief was to be responsible for all the land forces of the Crown, both at home and abroad. This included the right of appointing officers in the Militia, which had previously belonged to the Lords-Lieutenant of counties. Here again he was attacking privilege in the search for efficiency.

The British Army at this time (unlike the continental armies) attached to every General Officer two staff officers. This dualism reached its peak in the Adjutant-General and the Quartermaster-General, who were co-equal and rival authorities. Cardwell altered this and the Quartermaster-General at the War Office became an officer of the Adjutant-General's Department. Perhaps he had visions of a Chief of Staff, but that was something he dared not embark upon at this stage. By going too far or too fast he might wreck everything.

Cardwell next turned his attention to the conditions of service. How could the Army be made more attractive and at the same time more efficient? Until 1847, men were enlisted for twenty-one years' service with the colours—practically a life sentence. The period had been lowered to twelve years in 1847 but it was still too long, particularly when it is remembered that more than half this period was served abroad, usually in India or the tropics. After twelve such years a man's physique had usually deteriorated. The human problem gave point to a serious deficiency in Army organisation. Under such conditions of service it was impossible to form a reserve of well-trained and vigorous men, which the lessons of the Franco-Prussian War had made more than ever necessary. Cardwell's answer was six years with the colours and six in reserve. In spite of much criticism from senior officers—many of whom no doubt deplored the abolition of flogging, purchase, and other new-fangled ideas—the system worked.

In 1861 the Prince Consort had vainly pleaded with Palmerston that breech-loaders should be issued to the British Army. It remained for Cardwell some twelve years later to introduce the Martini-Henry rifle, the first satisfactory breech-loader to be used by British infantry.

Cardwell's abounding energy and initiative were next directed to the problem of regimental reorganisation. The old regiments of the line were known by numbers and for the most part lacked any territorial basis. Cardwell divided Great Britain and Ireland into sixty-five infantry regimental districts, each containing the depot of the regiment to be associated with its territory. Each of these county regiments was to comprise at least two battalions, with one, two, or three battalions of Militia and generally all the volunteer infantry belonging to the district. The object of attaching at least two battalions to each depot was that one should always be at the depot whilst the other was on foreign service. By alternating the foreign service of the battalions every few years it was possible to ensure that the units abroad consisted always of well-trained and seasoned men. Even Cardwell, however, had to keep his hands off the cavalry regiments; they were the stronghold of privilege and social influence. He did, however, increase the total of their establishments from 8,762 men to 10,422.

The artillery he treated in a similar fashion to the infantry, but the subdivision was imperfect by reason of the fact that the Royal Artillery continued to be worked as a single regiment. He increased its total of horsed guns from 180 to 336 and added some 5,000 men. But such was the conservatism of the ordnance officers that they actually insisted on going back to muzzle-loading cannon, thereby keeping us behind the rest of Europe for the best part of twenty years.

Cardwell left office with the fall of the Gladstone Government in 1874. He had increased the strength of the Army in the United Kingdom by 25 battalions, by 156 field-guns, and much equipment. The reserves available for foreign service had been raised from 3,545 to 35,905 men. These were great and measurable gains, but much of his work for the British Army, covering its organisation and conditions of service, cannot be tabulated and assessed. An amazing feature of all this was that Cardwell left the Estimates lower than he had found them! Much of his work was accomplished in spite of deep prejudice. What he could have achieved had he had the acquiescence, let alone the backing, of the

Commander-in-Chief is beyond reckoning. But that was not to be; the Duke of Cambridge fought progress with great tenacity, and with the Queen's support 'held on' until 1895. Suffice it to say that for the next twenty-five years the Army was a valuable asset in our diplomacy. As has already been indicated, Cardwell could not carry his reforms as far as he desired and perhaps the most serious flaw in his reorganisation was the lack of the formation of a proper General Staff, which was to prove a serious handicap in the South African campaign of 1899.

The Reform Bill of 1867 made the education of the masses a problem of urgency and in 1870 W. E. Forster introduced a Bill which provided a universal system of primary education for children under thirteen. It did not provide free education, because only those parents who could not afford payment were excused fees, but it was a great step forward. For the first time authority and responsibility were given to locally elected school boards, with powers to levy rates, build schools, provide teachers, and, if they thought fit, insist upon the attendance of all children who were not educated in any other way. Denominational schools were left untouched and grants were, in fact, increased, but no rate aid was allowed to them. Religious differences were still an obstacle to the smooth working of a national system of education, but the Forster Act of 1870 did provide that no children grew up without elementary education because their parents were poor.

One year later (in 1871) the cause of education made an important advance in another field. Gladstone's Government introduced and carried the University Tests Act, whereby the Universities of Oxford and Cambridge threw open for the first time all lay posts, in the Colleges as well as the Universities, to men of all creeds upon equal terms. That the battle to free Oxford and Cambridge from the bondage of Church monopoly should have been won under the leadership of so ardent a Churchman as Gladstone is evidence of his vision and courage.

We now turn to another great reform which is of particular interest in any study of the life and times of Haldane. Until 1873 England retained two legal systems side by side: the Common Law, administered in one set of courts; and Equity (which overrode it), administered in another. Lord Selborne's great Act of 1873 fused these two systems by providing that they should be administered concurrently in every court by every judge, and that, where their rules conflicted, the rules of Equity should prevail. Lord Selborne, however, went further: he re-modelled the courts themselves. At that time there were still three separate Common Law courts of unlimited jurisdiction, Queen's Bench, Common Pleas, and Exchequer. The only machinery which kept them at one was the court called the Exchequer Chamber, in which appeals from the judges of any of them were heard by judges of the other two. The Court of Chancery, which administered Equity, had since 1851 been regularly organised in two 'instances'—the first comprising the Lord Chancellor, the Master of the Rolls, and three Vice-Chancellors; the second, two Lord Justices sitting with the Lord Chancellor as a Court of Appeal. There were, in addition, three courts which dealt with special branches of the law: the High Court of Admiralty, the Court of Probate, and the Court of Divorce and Matrimonial Causes. From decisions in all these seven courts appeal in the final instance lay with the House of Lords. Lord Selborne's Act of 1873 united all seven courts to form one supreme court of judicature. The London Bankruptcy Court was left outside at the time but came in later. At first the old titles were retained and what had been separate courts became separate divisions, but by 1880 they were reduced (as had been intended) to the triple scheme which still obtains. Only in one respect did Lord Selborne's great work engender political agitation. He organised his supreme court in two 'instances'—a High Court and a Court of Appeal, and his Act abolished the appeal jurisdiction of the House of Lords. This alarmed the Peers, and when the Conservatives returned to power in 1874 Lord Cairns passed an amending Act in 1876 restoring final appeal to the House of Lords.

In February 1874, Gladstone's first Administration came to an end. It ranks as one of the greatest during the long reign of Queen Victoria. Gladstone was to be Prime Minister again three times but never was he to repeat the brilliant achievements of the years 1868–1874.

Disraeli, who for over twenty-five years had led the Conservative Party in the House of Commons with but three brief intervals in office between long periods in opposition, now found himself for the first time at the head of an Administration with an assured Parliamentary majority. But it was too late for this strange romantic genius to fulfil the brilliant promise of the long years in opposition. He was seventy years of age, and, before his long Ministry ended, the deadly pains of gout had sapped his physical and mental stamina. Old age and gout were poor equipments for supporting the exacting office of Prime Minister. But that was not all. In 1872 he had suffered a shattering loss in the death of his devoted wife. Whilst Disraeli had great influence with men and had many devoted followers, the springs of his happiness and contentment were derived from the society of women. After his wife's death he sought solace in a romantic friendship with two elderly sisters, the Countess of Bradford and the Dowager Countess of Chesterfield—and in an enhanced, almost fantastic, devotion to the Queen. But he was an old and lonely man and as his long Ministry moved forward his physical frailty increased.

Disraeli found too (as many before and since have done) that the freedom of opposition is a very different thing from the great responsibility of high office. He was a social reformer at heart, but few of his followers in Parliament supported him on that account. In opposition, however, he had attacked Gladstone's reforms up hill and down dale. That was part of the 'game' and superbly well he played it, but now in office he could hardly take reform as his primary *motif*. He had got to find another banner under which to fight. This he did, and one which was much in keeping with the heart and mind of this romantic figure—the Monarchy and the Empire.

Disraeli gathered together in his Cabinet (and outside) many outstanding men, the greatest being Lord Salisbury. Salisbury had left the Conservative front bench in 1867 in dislike of Disraeli's franchise extension, but was now induced to return as Secretary for India.

Whilst Disraeli did not place social reform in the forefront of his political programme, he was, as has already been mentioned, a reformer at heart and the session of 1875 was to witness the passage of some highly useful domestic legislation. Mention should be made of at least two. An Artisans Dwelling Act for the first time empowered local authorities to condemn, demolish, and reconstruct whole areas—an Act of which the radical Mayor of Birmingham, Joseph Chamberlain, was quick to take advantage. Another milestone of social reform was the great Public Health Act which remained the backbone of our sanitary law until 1937.

Before long Disraeli had an opportunity to display his unique powers in another field and one where his subtle, ingenious, and farsighted mind could have full play. In 1869 the Suez Canal had been opened and had changed the sea route from England to India. This placed Egypt in a strategic position of vital importance. Khedive Ismail owned about seven-sixteenths of the shares of the French Company which had constructed it. In December 1870, when Lord Granville was Foreign Secretary (in Gladstone's first Administration) and France was in the throes of the Franco-Prussian War, Ismail had not only offered to sell his interest to Great Britain but had suggested that she should buy up the whole of what was then a non-paying concern. This unique opportunity was rejected. Now once again the Khedive's financial straits drove him to seek a sale of his interest in the Company. In November 1875 he was negotiating with two French groups for the mortgage or sale of his shares, when the news that they were in the market reached the Foreign Office. At first it appeared that this 'second chance' was to be missed. The Foreign Office, presided over by the timid Lord Derby, thought nothing of the idea and it was only when the matter came before the Prime Minister that things took a different turn. Disraeli saw in a flash that the acquisition of these shares was not only likely to be of considerable financial value to this country (as proved to be the case) but that it had political value too. It was only, however, against strong opposition that he was able to secure Cabinet agreement. When it became known that the purchase had been made (for four million pounds) Disraeli's vision and leadership were acclaimed on all sides—even France and Germany professed approval!

Disraeli's imaginative genius soon discovered a new enterprise on which he could exercise his consummate skill. The Prince of Wales had just returned from a highly successful visit to India. This was surely the moment to capitalise the special glamour attaching to the monarchy for the Oriental mind. Disraeli proposed to add 'Empress of India' to the Queen's titles. As a result of this the Indian would, he held, regard the Sovereign not as a ruler of a distant and alien island but as Empress of his own country. There was in this proposal a deep understanding of the Oriental mind. After considerable opposition—much of it pedantic and unimaginative—the new title became law.

In August 1876, on the suggestion made by the Queen a month or two earlier, Disraeli was raised to the peerage as Earl of Beaconsfield. This was indeed a wise and timely proposal, for her illustrious Prime Minister's strength was slowly failing. His loss to the House of Commons was irreparable, but in the more sheltered atmosphere of the House of Lords it was possible for him to husband his strength whilst still continuing to give the country the benefit of his counsel.

The last phase of Disraeli's Administration was largely concerned with trouble in the Balkans—a long and complicated story indeed! Turkish misrule of the Christian races culminated in the Russo-Turkish War of 1877, to be followed by the Congress of Berlin in June and

July 1878. Disraeli was in his element in this imposing gathering of diplomats, and his powers of suave yet formidable bargaining were never seen to better advantage. It was indeed a superb performance and Disraeli returned from Berlin in triumph, bringing 'peace with honour' —a phrase re-coined by Disraeli from the reign of James I, when it was used by Robert Cecil. He was acclaimed by the Queen and by the people, and had he then dissolved Parliament (which had still two years to run), another seven-year mandate would almost certainly have been assured. He, however, risked the prolongation of his popularity over the longer term, but fate thereafter ceased to smile. He had passed the climax of his career.

Whilst the ageing Premier was engrossed with affairs in the Near East, matters at home were far from satisfactory. A trade decline had set in some three years earlier, to which was added an intense agricultural depression, largely engendered by competition from the development of the American prairies as grain lands within reach of the English and European markets. Germany and France retaliated by the imposition of tariffs, but the British Government took no action. Strange it was that Disraeli, who in 1846 had prophesied the ruin of agriculture as an inevitable result of free trade in corn and had been proved wrong for thirty years, was now, by reason of the emergence of the New World, suddenly right. Stranger still that he did nothing about it but allowed British agriculture to suffer irreparable damage. Perhaps it was evidence of a tired man that when a thirty-year-old prophecy proved true he was unable or unwilling to take advantage of it. Statesmen often regarded the fate of agriculture with some indifference. It was perhaps less politically dangerous because it did not produce the acute problems of unemployment which would be occasioned by the closure of a mine or a factory. The agricultural labourer could always slip away to the towns and find work there, or he could go overseas. Be that as it may, Disraeli's handling (or lack of handling) of this crisis showed a singular deficiency in his usual far-sightedness.

Economic discontent was, however, meat and drink to Gladstone in his attacks on his old foe, and the Opposition at Westminster began to look up. Other clouds, too, were drifting across the skies. 'Home Rule' for Ireland was launched, under the inspiration of Isaac Butt (who invented the phrase), at a Dublin meeting in 1870. In 1874 it carried some fifty-seven seats at the General Election. Butt was a good speaker and put his case before the House of Commons in a conciliatory and constitutional manner, but he was ignored and rebuffed. When in April 1877 his Party's annual Home Rule motion was defeated by 417 votes to 67, certain of Butt's following who preferred more dramatic methods sought control, and in 1878 he resigned the leadership and made way for them. The modest, conciliatory Butt was succeeded by Charles Stewart Parnell, a great political tactician whose meteoric career ended in tragedy. Parnell was the first politician to use the weapon of obstruction on a large scale, which he did with devastating effect. It could be fairly claimed that the barrenness of legislation during the later years of Disraeli's Administration was largely due to these particular tactics. Parnell's cause was greatly aided by the agricultural slump, which was desperate in Ireland and was aggravated and embittered by differences of religion and race. The relations between landlord and tenant had all the seeds of civil war. In such a climate the Irish National Land League was formed, with Parnell as President. Henceforward Irish revolutionary forces were attacking on two fronts, at Westminster and over the Irish countryside.

Serious as were these problems at home, Disraeli's Administration was even more deeply concerned in two disasters overseas—disasters which were to cause a reversal of that public opinion which had, little more than a year before, acclaimed Disraeli on his return from the Congress of Berlin. The ill-conceived Zulu War, with the tragic disaster at Isandhlwana (1879), was hardly likely to bring credit to Disraeli's imperialism, although it must be admitted that he was ill served by Lord Chelmsford (who commanded the British troops) and by Sir Bartle Frere (the High Commissioner), who committed his country to war contrary to instructions. A lesser man might, and with some justification, have used Chelmsford and Frere as scapegoats, but Disraeli was not cast in that mould; he defended both men in Parliament and did not recall either!

Disraeli's imperialistic policy suffered a further setback when the Afghan War, concluded by the Treaty of Gandamak, broke out afresh as a result of the massacre of the British Minister, his suite and escort at the Legation at Kabul (1879). Following so soon after the disaster at Isandhlwana, this deeply shocked public opinion.

Gladstone's anti-imperialistic agitation was greatly strengthened by these disasters and the veteran leader (then seventy years of age) 'stumped the country' with unabated passion and eloquence. The

Liberal forces were greatly heartened, but the Conservatives (misled by success at two by-elections) were far from realising that the tide was flowing against them. On the 8th of March 1880 Disraeli announced a dissolution, making Home Rule his principal issue. Economic discontent, a reaction against Disraeli's imperialist policy, and the Irish vote gave the Liberals a sweeping victory. Their majority in the House of Commons was 137 over the Conservatives, the Irish Nationalists winning 65 seats as a third Party.

The Conservative Cabinet resigned without meeting the new Parliament; the rule of Disraeli was over. He delivered his last notable speech in a debate on the evacuation of Kandahar on 9 March 1881. On April 19th he died. So ended a career of memorable splendour.

In 1880 (on the return of the Liberals to power) Haldane was twenty-four years of age. The preceding pages have briefly touched upon some of the outstanding political events and personalities of those years. No specific mention has been made of the Industrial Revolution in these pages, but its movement was ceaseless and its momentum showed no signs of slackening. It reached out into every branch of human endeavour. It was, in the words of Dr G. M. Trevelyan, 'by far the most important movement in social history since the Saxon conquest'.[1]

Before we resume the story, and in an endeavour to recapture the climate of those far-off days, we should examine some of the less spectacular but no less important features of Victorian England. Perhaps, too, we should try to discover what fundamental conditions governed the life and thought of those times.

Whilst it might well be said that the overriding feature of our life today is the fear of war, it would be equally true to say that it was the very absence of this fear which characterised the Victorian scene. This country had certainly been engaged in war on more than one occasion, but on so limited a scale and so far removed from these islands that it did little to upset the deep-rooted belief in inevitable progress. The record of achievement certainly gave some point to this belief. Material progress and social reforms blossomed in such a climate; but there was more to it than that, for they were rooted in a seriousness of thought and purpose which characterised Victorian England. The whole period was marked by a deep concern with religious questions, many regarding life (even politics) as a part of personal religion. It was this bond which

G. M. Trevelyan, *English Social History* (Longmans).

united Gladstone, an Anglo-Catholic, with his Nonconformist followers. The popular heroes of the seventies and eighties of the last century were men of deep religious conviction, Livingstone, Gordon, Shaftesbury, and Gladstone. They were very different from one another but they had this in common: they believed that life was the service of God. It is not suggested that the dogmas of Christianity were never challenged; they were, and that constantly, but the ethics of Christianity were generally accepted, even by the agnostic. Sir Robert Ensor cogently expresses this view in these words:[1]

No one will ever understand Victorian England who does not appreciate that among highly civilized, in contradistinction to more primitive, countries it was one of the most religious that the world has known. Moreover its particular type of Christianity laid a peculiarly direct emphasis upon conduct; for, though it recognized both grace and faith as essentials to salvation, it was in practice also very largely a doctrine of salvation by works.

The moral earnestness of the Victorians and an awakened social conscience found expression in far-reaching reforms, many of them long overdue. There remained, it is true, many dark spots in an England rapidly becoming industrialised, which privilege, power, and greed fought hard to retain; but these citadels were under constant attack, and if it remained for a later age to bring about their fall, it cannot be denied that the seeds of their dissolution were sown in the Victorian age.

It is sometimes suggested that the Victorians were smug and hypocritically pious. Such a charge cannot be entirely denied, but any objective review of the achievements of the Victorian age cannot fail to place such criticism in its true perspective. Smugness and hypocrisy are not the monopoly of any particular age; perhaps, however, they come to light more easily in a time of great achievement. The battle between those who consider that the Victorian age touched a peak of greatness never before achieved, and those (a dwindling minority) who believe that its outstanding qualities were hypocrisy, gloom, snobbery, and cruelty, still continues. Perhaps the claims of the eulogists are sometimes overstated, but on the record (black and white) it is surely unrealistic to seek to devalue the character and achievements of the Victorians as some would still wish to do.

Turning from these more general observations which apply to the Victorian age as a whole, we can the better assess the life and times of Haldane if we turn our attention to the cultural background of the

[1] Ensor, *England 1870–1914*.

years we have reviewed politically (1854–1880). Haldane was born in an age of great intellectual activity. Dr G. M. Trevelyan (in his *English Social History*) goes so far as to say that 'the world is not likely to see again so fine and broad a culture for many centuries to come'.

What memorable figures pass across the stage! Poetry could claim Tennyson, Browning, Swinburne, and Arnold. Prose was represented by, among others, Macaulay, Carlyle, Mill, Ruskin, and Spencer. The Victorian novel triumphed in Dickens, Thackeray, Trollope, and George Eliot. Science, too, could claim Darwin, Huxley, and Kelvin.

The list is far from complete and one could continue to name men and women who by their writings were influencing the mind and thought of the Victorians of the period we are now considering. Mr Frank Swinnerton in his recent book *Background with Chorus*, in commenting on H. G. Wells and Arnold Bennett, uses some words which are significant of the period now under review. He says, 'They belonged to the Victorian age and believed in sharing their knowledge. They were instinctive educationalists, tellers, explainers, helpers.' This diffusion of knowledge was a notable feature of the period, and how well Mr Swinnerton's words apply to Haldane!

But not in his reading alone was the Victorian widening and deepening his outlook. Material prosperity had made possible a great increase in foreign travel, and Englishmen were not only exploring the natural beauties of Switzerland but were finding delight in the architecture and the galleries of Italy and France. It is strange at first sight that, with this deepened interest in the arts, Victorian architecture was so deplorable. The blame would seem to lie with the advent of the Industrial Revolution. In spite of Ruskin and William Morris and their followers, who were untiring in their efforts to retain and develop beauty in daily life, craftsmanship declined and mechanisation took its place. The development of railways made it possible to transport standardised building materials from town to town, and local building material and craftsmanship were gradually supplanted.

Foreign musicians had for long found a warm welcome in this country: the names of Joachim, Clara Schumann, and Hans Richter deserve special mention for their important contribution to English taste in music. English musical composition, however, was in a sorry state, in spite of the great efforts made by Sterndale Bennett (who died in 1875), but in the 1870s there was something of a revival of music in England, largely due to the compositions and teaching of four men,

Parry, Stanford, Mackenzie, and Sullivan. Neither should the great work of Sir Charles Hallé, both as a pianist and a conductor, be forgotten. He it was who organised a permanent orchestra in Manchester and later took it on tour to Edinburgh, Leeds, Birmingham, and other cities. Nor should it be overlooked that the 'musical evening' was a feature of Victorian social life. The standard attained may not have been very high but it provided endless enjoyment for performer and audience alike. There were, too, theatres and music-halls in abundance which catered for the Englishman's age-long love of acting and the actor.

Not only were the intellectual and cultural tastes of countless men and women being stimulated as never before (and this quite apart from the lighter side of entertainment), but with the rise of a great middle-class society organised games developed in a remarkable way. The English landed gentry could still have their shooting, fishing, hunting, and horse-racing, but cricket, football, and lawn tennis were to become the games of the people—a development which has perhaps turned too sharply in the direction of watching rather than playing.

The laws of Association football were formulated in 1863 and the first real International match was played between England and Scotland in 1872. Rugby football (in vogue at Rugby School) extended its borders when the senior London Rugby Club (Blackheath) was founded in 1860 and achieved universal recognition on the formation of the English Rugby Union in 1871, in which year the first International was played between England and Scotland.

Cricket (the word was first used in 1598) had long before the period we are now considering entered the professional stage, but it was an amateur, Dr W. G. Grace, then at the zenith of his prowess, who stimulated 'cricket watching' during the period 1870–1886, until it became a craze. In 1878 the spectators were to have the added thrill of witnessing the first Test Match against the Australians.

Lawn tennis ('invented' by a Major Wingfield in 1874 under the name of Sphairistike) was 'taken over' by a committee of the Wimbledon All England Croquet and Lawn Tennis Club in 1877, and rules were adopted which have changed little since those far-off days. Tennis became a most popular game for men and women of almost all ages and so it remains.

It might be argued, and with some truth, that a considerable proportion of the population enjoyed little of this larger and fuller life.

On the other hand it is equally true to say that the area of progress and enlightenment was expanding year by year. Perhaps most significant of all was the rise of a great middle-class population which in the course of time was to enter into a great and richly deserved inheritance.

This is not the place to roam over the whole field of human endeavour which found so fertile a soil in the Victorian age; everywhere there was movement, some of it confused and ill-directed but all contributing to one of the greatest periods in our history. The intention of the foregoing pages has been to present a brief historical 'backcloth' covering the period between Haldane's birth in 1856 and his active interest in politics, which might be said to have begun in 1880, although he did not enter the House of Commons until 1885. Thenceforward he himself was to play an increasingly important part in the life of his country, and it is hoped that the story of this man—his work, his hopes, his tragedy, his courage—will carry forward the wider story briefly sketched in the preceding pages. Before we reach that point, however, what of the years between 1856 and 1880 in so far as they concern Haldane personally?

CHAPTER I

Scottish Inheritance

*It is a reverend thing to see an ancient castle or
building not in decay, or to see a fair timber
tree sound and perfect; how much more to
behold an ancient family which hath stood
against the waves and weathers of time.*

General Sir Aylmer Haldane in the introduction to his book *The
Haldanes of Gleneagles* quotes these words of Bacon and adds how
peculiarly applicable they are to the family of Haldane of Gleneagles,
a family which 'for more than 700 years has continued without a break
in the direct male line, and its senior representative possesses today the
same lands which his ancestor acquired in the twelfth century'. Certainly the Haldanes were people of character and on more than one
occasion 'stood against the waves and weathers of time' in marked
degree.

It is difficult to decide how far one should retrace one's steps to
discover or speculate on the part played by heredity in the formation
of a man's character. As this is not a treatise on the Haldanes of Gleneagles (already so admirably accomplished), perhaps we may be
satisfied by first considering Richard Burdon Haldane's grandfather
and great-uncle, James Alexander Haldane (1768–1851) and Robert
Haldane of Airthrey (1764–1842). The story of these two remarkable
men will have, I believe, some value when we come to consider the
life and character of their illustrious descendant.

James Alexander, who had lost both parents while still a boy and was
brought up by his uncles, was destined for the sea and at the age of
seventeen sailed for India in the service of the East India Company.
In 1793, at the age of twenty-five, he was given command of the
Melville Castle, a ship in which the Haldane family had a third interest.

The captain of an East Indiaman was also a trading agent of the Company and the financial outlook for James was bright indeed. In the same year he married Mary, only child and heiress of Major Joass of Colleonard, County Banff, and in January 1794 joined the *Melville Castle* at Portsmouth. Circumstances delayed the sailing of the fleet of East Indiamen, which consisted of twenty-five ships, and not until May 1794 did it weigh anchor. It was during this interval that an incident occurred which indicated the character and courage of James Haldane:

For some time the crew of one of the ships of the fleet, the *Dutton*, had shown increasing signs of discontent, for which there appear to have been good reasons, and by the middle of March the spirit of the men had become definitely mutinous and the captain applied to His Majesty's ship *Regulus* for help. On the evening of March 19 a lieutenant with a boat's crew from the *Regulus* came alongside and demanded the surrender of the ringleaders, whereupon the men got up round-shot on deck and threatened to sink the first boat which came alongside. The lieutenant of the *Regulus* then withdrew and the captain of the *Dutton* left his ship, under the impression that this would quiet the men, who on the contrary grew more and more excited, and their officers lost all control of them. At this moment, when the men were threatening to blow up the ship, Captain James Haldane of the *Melville Castle* appeared alongside in his boat, to be greeted with shouts of 'Keep off or we will sink you'. Undeterred Captain James took his boat round by the stern, and in a few minutes he had scrambled up to the quarter-deck. There his first act was to restore confidence to the officers, his next to refuse to lead an attack on the mutineers. Instead he began to reason calmly with the men, asking what they imagined they could do in the presence of twenty ships of the line. This had an immediate effect, but seeing that there were still signs of confusion and uneasiness amongst the men, he learned that some of the ringleaders were still bent on blowing up the ship. He went down at once to the magazine, and there found two men, both drunk and both swearing to send themselves and their comrades either to heaven or hell. One of them was in the act of wrenching the iron bars from the door and the other had a shovelful of live coals ready to throw into the magazine. Haldane put a pistol to the head of the man at the door and told him that if he stirred he was a dead man. Calling at once for irons, as if disobedience was out of the question, he saw them placed on both men and the mutiny was quelled.[1]

All seemed set for a highly successful career in the service of the East India Company, but other and even more powerful forces were at work in the direction of James Haldane's life. His marriage had certainly made him less attracted to life at sea, but his decision to retire from the service was largely a religious one. He and his elder brother Robert had come under the powerful influence of the Evangelical Movement.

Robert (Richard Burdon Haldane's great-uncle) desired in boyhood

[1] Maj.-Gen. Sir F. Maurice, *Haldane, 1856–1915* (Faber and Faber).

to prepare himself for the ministry in the Church of Scotland, but in those days it was considered inappropriate for one of his fortune and position to become a minister and he eventually decided in 1780 to join the Royal Navy—he was then in his seventeenth year. He first served in H.M.S. *Monarch* (commanded by his uncle, Captain Duncan) and was then transferred to H.M.S. *Foudroyant* and took part in the celebrated and successful action against the French ship *Pégase* in April 1781. His courage and skill on that occasion were noted by Captain Jervis (later to become Lord St Vincent) and he indicated his approval by appointing Haldane to accompany one of the lieutenants to take possession of the *Pégase* and to bring back her commander, Le Chevalier de Cillart. This delicate operation was successfully accomplished, largely by reason of Haldane's courtesy, tact, and determination, and his ability to speak French! After the action Sir John Jervis wrote to Haldane's uncle, Captain Duncan, congratulating him on the courage and ability of his nephew and predicting a great future in the Royal Navy for him. His renown, however, was to be gained elsewhere. Haldane continued to serve in the *Foudroyant* under Captain Jervis and took part in the relief of Gibraltar. On her return to England the *Foudroyant* paid off and Sir John Jervis was appointed to H.M.S. *Salisbury*. Preparations were made for a voyage round the world for purposes of discovery, coupled with an attack on the Spanish settlements in South Africa. Captain Jervis expressly selected young Robert Haldane to accompany him, having had ample evidence of his reliability, courage, and initiative. Peace put an end to the South African expedition and Sir John Jervis for a time retired into private life. Haldane remained in the Navy for a short while longer, but as the prospect of immediate promotion appeared unlikely he left the service, married, and settled down as a country gentleman on his property at Airthrey. Before he left the Royal Navy, however, he had come under the influence of Dr David Bogue, a Scottish minister at Gosport, and it may well be that his decision to retire from the Navy was in some measure influenced by the growing conviction that he must spend his life and substance for the benefit and enlightenment of mankind. He passed some fifteen years managing and improving the estate and then in 1798 he sold Airthrey to General Sir Robert Abercromby, an uncle of his brother's wife. His object is so doing was to obtain funds to go to India to spread the Gospel. This he was prevented from doing owing to the opposition of the Directors of the East India Company.

At this point the two brothers joined forces. Robert, through a weakness of the throat, was himself unable to preach to any great extent, but James, who possessed a fine voice and great natural gifts as a preacher, was soon conducting an evangelistic mission throughout the Highlands and the remote islands of Scotland. The elder brother spent large sums in the furtherance of the work (in all about £100,000) and, besides erecting churches and 'tabernacles' throughout the country, established a theological seminary for preparing evangelists. Both brothers wrote many theological works and commentaries on the Bible, and in spite of considerable opposition and misrepresentation continued their evangelistic work by word and pen with courage and determination.

Robert died on 12 December 1842, survived by Catherine his wife and an only child. James died on 6 February 1851 in his eighty-third year. He married twice and had no fewer than fifteen children. Of the two brothers it was said:[1]

Both were content for a time to be sneered at by the world and accounted madmen for the sake of Christ. Both dedicated intellectual talents of no common order to the same cause. The one by preaching, but still more by his writings; the other by his writings, but far more by his preaching, taught and vindicated the same great truths. In all their undertakings for the promotion of religion they advanced with united zeal and strength. Although each was distinguished for a determined will, strong individuality of character, and a strict adherence to his own views of duty, there subsisted between them a remarkable harmony of design and oneness of spirit; and never during their long and honourable course of mutual co-operation was there one jarring feeling to disturb their efforts for the common object they so consistently pursued. That object was the glory of Christ and the salvation of their fellow-men; and now that the career of both is closed, and death has affixed his seal on the record of their earthly labours, the simplicity of their holy aim, the depth of their hallowed benevolence, and the steadfastness of their lofty principles stand more plainly revealed. From the moment they undertook to devote their lives to labour in the Gospel, there was no looking back to scenes of past enjoyment. Wealth, honour, worldly renown, and reputation were all counted but loss; nor did the seductive hope of earning a name and a place in the Christian world ever tempt ambition. Their single aim was wholly to follow the Lord.

Such were the grandfather and great-uncle of Richard Burdon Haldane.

James Haldane's third son, Robert, was born at Edinburgh on 27 January 1805. He was educated at the Edinburgh High School and Geneva. On his return home he studied law at Edinburgh University and became a Writer to the Signet. He was a shrewd and successful man of business but his main interests, like those of his father and uncle,

[1] Alexander Haldane, *The Lives of Robert and James Alexander Haldane of Airthrey.*

were religious. His missionary zeal, as also his rigid Calvinistic theology, was rather more unobtrusive than theirs but certainly no less sincere. 'He was very devout,' his son Richard writes in his *Autobiography*, 'and had fitted up a barn where he used once a fortnight to preach to a considerable audience of old-fashioned Scottish country folk who came to hear the Word of God in all its strictness. On alternate Sundays he used to ride miles to various villages and preach there.'

Robert Haldane, who purchased Cloan, in Perthshire, about 1852, loved a simple country life and was never happier than when he could escape from Edinburgh to Cloan. All animals were his friends and it is pleasant to picture this somewhat austere figure feeding the pigeons that lit on his shoulders, and encouraging the horses and ponies to nose his pockets for the bread he carried there for them.

Robert Haldane married in 1841 Janet Makgill, daughter of John Makgill of Kemback in the County of Fife, and by her he had six children. She died in childbirth in February 1851. On 27 July 1853 he married as his second wife Mary Elizabeth, daughter of Richard Burdon-Sanderson of West Jesmond, Northumberland, a great-niece of Lord Chancellor Eldon and of the great jurist and judge Lord Stowell. Richard Burdon-Sanderson had a distinguished career at Oxford, where he was the contemporary of Keble. His daughter in her reminiscences of her early days writes that 'he there [at Oxford] became very much concerned about divine things, used to attend early services and indeed never allowed anything to stand in the way of his presence at chapel twice a day'. As time went on, Richard Burdon-Sanderson became more and more immersed in the writing of religious pamphlets, and the narrow Evangelism which he finally embraced cast a deep shadow over an otherwise happy home. He had joined the Plymouth Brethren in 1837. He was a correspondent and friend of James Alexander Haldane and no doubt the identity of their religious creeds commended Robert Haldane to him as a suitor for his daughter's hand, the more so as he found in Robert one who had inherited much of his father's active interest in religion.

The first child of the marriage, a boy, died in infancy. The second, Richard Burdon, was born at 17 Charlotte Square, Edinburgh, on 30 July 1856. Robert Haldane was over fifty when his second son was born. His mind and outlook were already set within the narrow confines of the Calvinism he had inherited from his father and uncle. The relationship between father and son was an affectionate one but there was no deep understanding between them. It should not, however, be thought that Robert Haldane had no influence on his son, albeit that influence was often negative and restrictive.

Mary Elizabeth Haldane, who was some twenty years younger than her husband, was a remarkable woman. Whilst she shared many of her husband's religious views, she had a deeper understanding and wider sympathy with those whose faith was of a different order. She herself had experienced religious doubts and perplexities in her youth. With the passing of the years her spiritual stature developed and her remarkable personality played an important part in the life of her son. Their intense devotion to each other (which found expression not least in a daily letter from 1877 until her death in 1925 at the great age of 100) came to be regarded as a classic of devotion between a mother and son. It undoubtedly brought them both a great deal of happiness, but whether it was an unmixed blessing to Richard Haldane might be questioned. In reading the many thousands of letters—some written only a few hours after a visit to Cloan—one wonders a little whether a self-imposed task, albeit a task of delight, begun in 1877 could be happily and profitably sustained for some forty-seven years, particularly when it is remembered that the writer during many of those years was an immensely busy lawyer and politician. On the other hand it might well be that Haldane sustained his labour of love on a two-fold basis. In the first place he realised how much pleasure his mother derived from these letters, particularly as the years advanced and she became increasingly tied to Cloan; and secondly they held the seeds of a diary, which was so much a feature of Victorian and Edwardian times. When one is considering these letters there is another aspect that calls for comment. It might well be thought that the picture presented of Haldane in them is of a rather self-satisfied and self-laudatory individual. It must be remembered, however, that these letters were from a son to his mother. She naturally longed for news of her son's achievements and successes, and he responded without reserve. They were not written with one eye to future publication and to that extent they are all the more interesting and valuable.

Richard Haldane never married and his mother remained the most powerful feminine influence in his life.

CHAPTER 2

Edinburgh–Göttingen–London: 1856–1879

The Haldane family divided their time between the fine Adam house in Charlotte Square and Cloan, a comparatively small estate which Robert Haldane had purchased as a summer home. It lies some few miles to the east of Auchterarder and adjoins the estate of Gleneagles, which had been in the Haldane family for many centuries. The view from the house to the Grampians covered a lovely strip of Perthshire, and the estate itself, with its burns and pools, was a fisherman's paradise.

The children of Robert Haldane's first marriage soon went their ways, and ere long Charlotte Square and Cloan were echoing to the voices of the five surviving children of his second marriage. They were Richard, the eldest, George (born 1858), John (born 1860), Elizabeth (born 1862), and the youngest, William (born 1864). George died of diphtheria when he was 16, leaving the memory, long cherished, of a singularly lovely character. His sensitive nature found expression in an untroubled religious faith, a great love of music, and an endearing sense of humour. There was in 'Geordie' a lightness and brightness of texture not evident in other members of the family. John, Elizabeth, and William all achieved considerable distinction with the passing of the years and all survived their brother Richard, to whom they were devoted. The sense of 'family' was strong and lasting. Robert Haldane had by the time of his second marriage built up a fine business and was highly regarded in legal circles in Edinburgh. Perforce much time had to be spent there, but it was Cloan which drew them and became increasingly the centre of their life and happiness.

Life in Edinburgh for the Haldane children contained few excitements and they were happiest when left to the comparative freedom of the nursery—it was there they lived their real lives. In these early years even their love for their parents was tinged with awe. Those were not the days when children mingled happily with their elders; much was

41

left to the authority and guidance of a nurse, who could bring happiness or misery into so many young lives. This important personage in the Haldane household commanded a wage of £25 a year—paid half-yearly—and twice a year she made an expedition to the savings bank and another to the post office in order to put money in the bank and send home a money order! Her name was Betsy Ferguson, a woman of little education but considerable character and intelligence. She had great influence with the Haldane children and, as often happens with a devoted nurse, she enjoyed prophesying the future careers of her small charges. On a visit to London with Richard, then aged about six, they went on a sight-seeing expedition to the Houses of Parliament. In the House of Lords she deposited him on the Woolsack, saying 'the bairn will sit there some day as of right'.

Life at Cloan provided a greater opportunity for the young people to get to know their parents better and was less restricted than in Edinburgh. There was riding, fishing, and shooting, and a lovely countryside to explore. As has already been indicated, Robert Haldane loved all animals and something of that love was acquired by his eldest son; particularly was this true of his devotion to dogs. Richard Haldane became a good shot and enjoyed a day on the moors with his gun, but as the years slipped by he loved most the long tramps over the hills with a friend or alone except for the companionship of his dog. Haldane was a great walker and could set and sustain the pace covering many miles, even when living in London and out of training.

Robert and Mary Haldane held, as has already been noted, deep religious convictions, and whilst in the course of time their children were in large measure to reject the orthodox teaching of their child-hood, they never lost that serious-mindedness which had been a family trait of the Haldanes for many generations.

Unfortunately there are few records of Richard Haldane's childhood. A hundred years ago people were unconcerned with the thoughts and dreams of a child. Maybe an affectionate mother or nurse might give passing thought to such things, but the record concerning Richard Haldane is meagre in the extreme and would certainly disappoint the appetite of a modern psycho-analyst.

At the age of eight Richard went to a preparatory school in Edin-burgh and a year or two later to Edinburgh Academy. It was here that he began to question in his own mind the narrow Calvinistic theology held by his father and to a somewhat lesser extent by his mother. The principal master at the Academy was a remarkable personality and a fine scholar, Dr James Clyde (whose son and grandson both became Lord President of the Court of Session). Dr Clyde was a Stoic and a passionate seeker after truth, two qualities which were to appear in marked degree in his young pupil's character in later life. One of Dr Clyde's duties was to read the Old Testament with his class and, while setting himself to avoid disturbing the faith of his pupils, he could not help letting them see that he himself did not accept what the Old Testament narratives recorded. This was not lost on Richard Haldane and ere long he was seeking an answer to the persistent questions which his parents' theology did nothing to explain.

From Edinburgh Academy, Haldane entered the University of Edinburgh at the age of sixteen. He found there many to stimulate his already enquiring mind. He studied Latin under W. Y. Sellar and English literature under David Masson, two inspiring teachers. Of equal or greater importance, he joined the students' Philosophical Society, taking an active part in its deliberations and meeting a number of young men who, like Haldane, were themselves seeking an answer to their questionings. He made a number of friends, and one in particular, Andrew Seth, afterwards Professor Seth Pringle-Pattison, with whom in after years he was to collaborate in producing a volume called *Essays in Philosophical Criticism*, dedicated to the memory of T. H. Green. It was Pringle-Pattison who was entrusted by the British Academy to write the memorial tribute to Haldane on his death in 1928.

Haldane was a voracious reader and already his mind was moving towards 'idealism' in philosophy through the writings of T. H. Green and Edward Caird. Of importance, too, was his friendship with Hutchison Stirling, the author of *The Secret of Hegel*. These were intellectually stimulating days in Edinburgh and Haldane was not slow to seize the opportunity of meeting men of culture, not only in the field of philosophy, which interested him especially, but in more general realms of thought. Here he owed much to the kindness of Professor Sellar, who would ask Haldane to his house when he was entertaining such men as Jowett and Matthew Arnold. Haldane in his *Autobiography* remembers Sellar in this moving passage:

It was the *De Rerum Natura* of Lucretius that fascinated me most, when I heard Sellar lecturing on it. It is more than fifty years since I listened while he declaimed to us his favourite passages. The lines at the beginning of the Second Book still remain in my memory, and I often repeat them to myself when alone:

'Sed nil dulcius est, bene quam munita tenere
Edita doctrinâ sapientum templa serena,
Despicere unde queas alios passimque videre
Errare atque viam palantis quaerere vitae,
Certare ingenio, contendere nobilitate,
Noctes atque dies niti praestante labore
Ad summas emergere opes rerumque potiri.'[1]

That was his creed, and it has ever since I heard him been mine also. I think that I
have in the main followed Leonardo da Vinci in the faith that it is even better to know
than to be.

Haldane was an active member of the Philomathic Society of the
University and a contemporary, Mr Charles A. Salmond, has left this
glimpse of him. 'He was distinguished even then by the acuteness of his
reasoning and the imperturbability of his temper. His urbanity could
not be disturbed by any number of noisy and mocking interruptions.'

During these years at the University, Haldane's religious faith was
deeply disturbed. Could the beliefs of his parents, which he himself had
previously accepted, stand up to reasonable examination? He sought an
answer in such books as *Old Faith and the New* by Strauss, and Renan's
Life of Jesus, but they merely enlarged the area of his doubt. He turned
to ministers of religion whom he knew but they could offer him little
help, for, to use Haldane's own words, 'they had not themselves gone
deeply enough down'. So his naturally philosophic turn of mind was
stimulated.

At this point in his life a somewhat strange but far-reaching decision
was taken by his parents. Robert and Mary Haldane had planned
to send their eldest surviving son to Balliol College, Oxford, but
they were tormented by the fear of the influence of the Anglican
Church atmosphere in Oxford. They therefore accepted an alternative
proposal that Richard should go to the German University of Göttingen. Among the men from whom Richard Haldane had sought
guidance in his perplexities was John Stuart Blackie, Professor of Greek
at Edinburgh. Blackie, a man of imagination and vision, could not
answer the young man's problems but he believed he could introduce
him to one who could. That man was Professor Lötze of Göttingen,

---

[1] Lucretius, ii.7. H. A. J. Munro's translation (adapted):

'But sweeter far to dwell remote, aloof
In some high mansion, built on Wisdom's hill:
Thence watch the errant crowd go to and fro,
Matching their wits, striving for precedence,
Toiling and moiling, hurrying night and day,
To rise to fortune and possess the world.'

one of the greatest and most spiritual German thinkers of that day. Blackie, it seems, was able to persuade Haldane's Calvinistic parents that the philosophy of Lötze was preferable to the Anglican Church atmosphere of Oxford—certainly no mean performance! What fascinating paths of speculation are opened up had Haldane indeed gone to Balliol and come under the powerful influence of Benjamin Jowett!

So it was that in April 1874, at the end of his second winter at Edinburgh University, he spent the summer semester at Göttingen. It was a strange new world for this lad of seventeen, but he was fortunate in finding a kind and understanding friend in Fräulein Schlote, with whom he took lessons in German. She was a most accomplished woman and the friendship formed in 1874 was to continue until Fräulein Schlote died shortly after the First World War.

Hermann Lötze, to whom Haldane bore a letter of introduction from Blackie, made a deep impression on him. The quiet, reserved old man saw the nature of the crisis through which his young pupil was passing and was able to guide him in his search for truth. Some thirty-six years later Haldane was to pay a noble tribute to Lötze in an address on 'The Soul of a People' in these words:

Göttingen was in these days full of great men. Yet the figure that stood out above all the others was that of my old master, Hermann Lötze. I had the privilege, boy as I was, of seeing him often in his study, as well as listening in his lecture-room, and to the end of my life I shall hold the deep impression he made on me—of a combination of intellectual power and the highest moral stature. It seems to me but yesterday that he used quietly to enter the lecture-room where we students sat expectant, and, taking his seat, fix his eyes on space as though he were looking into another world remote from this one. The face was worn with thought, and the slight and fragile figure with the great head looked as though the mind that tenanted it had been dedicated to thought and to nothing else. The brow and nose were wonderfully chiselled, the expression was a combination of tolerance with power. The delivery was slow and quiet, but the command of language was impressive. Our feeling towards him, as we sat and listened, was one of reverence mingled with affection.

It is interesting and significant to note that whilst the influence of Lötze on Haldane was profound in that it stimulated his search for truth and enlarged his vision in that search, it was not Lötze's philosophy which ultimately captured his allegiance. Much of Lötze's work was indeed a protest against the extravagant claims of Hegelian idealism, which Haldane was to embrace. A great teacher may, indeed, influence his pupil profoundly (as in this instance) without gaining a disciple.

Haldane took a modest part in the student life at Göttingen, but characteristically he was not deflected from the purpose with which he had gone there. He studied philosophy and a certain amount of theology and was instructed to read Fichte, Bishop Berkeley, Kant, and Hegel—strong meat for a young man of seventeen. Of equal importance were the long discussions he had with Lötze—a valuable corollary to his reading of the masters.

Haldane returned to Cloan in August 1874 so altered in appearance that his family hardly recognised him. He had let his hair grow long, had cultivated a moustache, and had become very thin. An even greater change had taken place in his mind. Gone was the depression which only three short months before had almost overwhelmed him. His own words describe his new outlook. 'My attention had become concentrated on a search for light about the meaning of God, Freedom and Immortality. Lötze had set me to pursue the search in a new spirit and with fuller consciousness of the vast theoretical obscurity in which these subjects were buried.'

Haldane never returned to the religious beliefs of his early youth, nor indeed did he subscribe to any orthodox creed thereafter. Perhaps Professor Seth Pringle-Pattison best described his friend's position when he wrote: 'He philosophised to satisfy a religious need, and the philosophic conclusions in which he rested were held by him with all the intensity which religious convictions possess for the ordinary man.' He always retained, however, a deep respect for the religious beliefs of others and was eager to discuss the ultimate nature of things with his friends. In later years he found particular delight in his friendship with the two Archbishops, Randall Davidson and Cosmo Lang, and, perhaps most of all, with W. R. Inge, Dean of St Paul's.

During the two years that remained of his Arts Course at Edinburgh University, Haldane gave himself with increased vigour but a lighter heart to his studies. He was fortunate to come under the influence of Campbell Fraser, the Professor of Logic and Metaphysics, who had just completed his monumental editions of Berkeley's Life and Works. Campbell Fraser was a stimulating teacher and was able to continue and enlarge the studies which Haldane had begun at Göttingen. It is still currently believed that Haldane's university education was mainly at Göttingen, and during the First World War, when every shade of connexion with Germany was hailed as evidence of a traitor, Haldane's sojourn in the German city was valuable fuel. As a student he left for

Göttingen in April 1874 and returned to Edinburgh in August 1874—a sojourn of some five months!

Before Haldane graduated in April 1876 two events at home were to occur which affected him profoundly. Richard's father and mother were, as already described, Calvinistic in theology, and Robert Haldane, if not his wife, a convinced Baptist. None of the children had been baptized in infancy but Robert and Mary Haldane were deeply anxious that Richard should accept adult baptism. Richard Haldane's attitude and response to their entreaties can best be described in his own words.

I took the view that the mere ceremony, though I would rather have avoided it, mattered little among people whose custom as citizens was to be baptised, provided one assented to no formula and gave no undertaking. My parents' anxiety was more to me than my own reluctance, and if, but only if, this anxiety could be relieved on terms that did not compromise me, I was willing to undergo the ceremony. My father did not, I think, realise in the least how far away from each other our minds were on foundational questions. He proposed that the ceremony should be gone through quite privately at the church to which the family went when in Edinburgh, and that no one should be present excepting those immediately concerned. I do not think that he had taken in the importance which I attached to this undertaking. Anyhow, he seemed to have let the appointment be known, for, when I got to the church, there were present not only the minister, but a crowd of deacons and other onlookers. My mind was at once made up. To begin with, I told them all openly that I would not refuse to go through the ceremony, but that I should make a definite explanation the moment it was over. I rose dripping from the font, and, facing the congregation, announced to them that I had consented to go through what had taken place only to allay the anxiety of my parents, but that now, as those present might have misunderstood, I must say something to them. It was that I could not accept their doctrines; that I regarded what had taken place as the merest external ceremony; and that for the future I had no connection with the church, or its teaching, or with any other church. I then changed my clothes and walked away from the building. There was much consternation, but nothing was said, probably because there was nothing to say.

Nothing could have been better designed to widen the theological chasm which existed between Richard Haldane and his father than this event. It says a great deal for their mutual affection that it survived this unhappy experience. We retain, and rightly so, great sympathy for those who cannot accept the narrow theology of their parents, as was the case with Haldane. Perhaps, however, we fail to try to understand the tormenting fear of those who are held in such theological subjection —fear that those they love are in fact 'sinning against the light'. Such bitterness of experience is classically portrayed in Edmund Gosse's *Father and Son*.

The other event was of a very different character. It was the death of George, Richard's younger brother. The affection which 'Geordie' inspired was of a special kind. With his sensitive, artistic nature and his sense of humour, he brought a lightness and gaiety of touch into this rather solemn household which could ill be spared. This anniversary was never to be forgotten by Richard and his mother, as his letters to her over nearly fifty years indicate.

In April 1876, Haldane graduated M.A. with First Class Honours in Philosophy (being the only student in his year to do so) and in the same year he carried off the Ferguson Philosophic Scholarship, open to the four Scottish Universities. During the winter that followed he began the study of law in the offices of two well-known Edinburgh firms of Writers to the Signet—Tods, Murray & Jamieson, and Drummond & Reid—with the first for conveyancing and feudal law, with the second for the mercantile side of legal business. At the same time he went to London as occasion demanded to eat dinners at Lincoln's Inn. His powers of sustained work were even then prodigious.

Haldane's father died in 1877 at the age of seventy-two, and for some time thereafter a good deal devolved upon the eldest son of his second marriage. John, the second surviving son, was already engrossed in the biological and physiological studies which ultimately brought him fame and honour. Such, however, was the range of his powers that a few years later (in 1883) he and his brother Richard jointly contributed an essay on the relation of philosophy to science, which appeared in the volume *Essays in Philosophical Criticism* edited by Seth Pringle-Pattison and Richard Haldane. John Scott Haldane was indeed a philosopher as well as a scientist.

William, the youngest brother, became an eminent Writer to the Signet and was Crown Agent for Scotland for many years. As the years passed and Richard's interests enlarged and his fame increased, it was William who relieved him of much of the burden of attending to his private affairs.

Elizabeth, the only daughter of Robert Haldane's second marriage, developed a striking personality and a fine mind. She, like her brothers Richard and John, wrote on philosophy, and in addition a history of nursing and a life of George Eliot and other books. She devoted much of her life to caring for her mother and her brother Richard, but characteristically found time to do much else besides, particularly in the field of education.

When things had settled down after Robert Haldane's death, Richard went to live in London, first in rooms in St Petersburg Place, off the Bayswater Road. He had been destined from the first for the Bar and, like many a young man from north of the Tweed, he came to London to try his fortune. The way was not made easy for Richard Haldane. He had little money and in London none of the friends that the promising young barrister makes at his public school and university. He had, moreover, a poor voice and few of the social graces which make a young man known and popular. He had, however, a fine mind and a tremendous capacity for work. It would, I think, be true to say that Haldane's finer and subtler qualities came to him through his mother, but his tenacity of purpose and calmness of spirit in all adversity were Haldane characteristics.

He went first into the chambers of William Barber in Old Square, Lincoln's Inn, where he read Equity drafting and conveyancing. Barber was a leading Junior on the Chancery side with a large practice and he soon found that young Haldane, besides being willing to work at all hours of the day and night, had a retentive memory and could recall cases he had studied and even the volumes in which they were recorded. The result was that Barber, who was grossly overworked, turned over to his young pupil difficult cases on which an opinion had been sought, it being Haldane's duty to write a draft for Barber's consideration. Haldane could have had no better training and he revelled in it. Soon after his arrival in London he wrote to his sister:

Court begins to sit to-morrow and we expect to be very busy. Indeed, Mr. Barber's wig has been airing before the fire for the last two days and we expect a shoal of briefs. His chambers consist of five rooms, one for himself, where I sit and work with him, in the absence of the chief devil, and in the other two sit the barristers and un-called members who work for him, and junior clerks of whom I am one. When Ingham, the chief junior barrister, returns he will sit beside Barber, and I shall move out into the next room beside Burnell, Lady Pine's nephew, who is a tall dark young man of seven and twenty. The clerk, who gives out opinions and drafts when Barber approves them, or burns them when he doesn't, which at times is the case, sits in a den at the door of the chambers to receive briefs and cases for opinion. He also makes tea for Mr. Barber and any one else who wants it, but as he is not skilful I get it elsewhere.

In those days he had little social life, although he did take some dancing lessons in company with Mrs Elizabeth Garrett Anderson, a grave and distinguished member of the medical profession. But Haldane's dancing days were of short duration and his only form of relaxation was—more work!

About this time Haldane moved from St Petersburg Place to rooms in Bruton Street. When he was not working in Barber's chambers he was reading at home—law, philosophy, and political economy. He even wrote short reviews of books for John Chapman (1822–1894), who was still editor of *The Westminster Review*, then approaching the end of its famous history.

Haldane learnt a great deal of Equity from Barber, but after a year in his chambers he wished to study Common Law, and on the introduction of Farrer Herschell, Mrs Burdon-Sanderson's[1] brother and later Lord Chancellor, he entered as a pupil with Lumley Smith, a busy Junior with chambers in King's Bench Walk. Lumley Smith had heard of Haldane from Barber and used him in very much the same way. He passed him the difficult cases to look into and very soon Haldane was acquiring a good knowledge of Common Law. At the same time Haldane's knowledge of Equity was useful to Lumley Smith.

Haldane remained at King's Bench Walk until he was called to the Bar in the autumn of 1879. He then took chambers (in the form of a garret!) at 5 New Square, Lincoln's Inn.

---

[1] Mrs Burdon-Sanderson was Richard Haldane's aunt by marriage. Her husband (Mrs Haldane's brother) was the eminent physiologist who later became Sir John Burdon-Sanderson.

CHAPTER 3

Law and Politics: 1880–1889

The story of the young barrister anxiously awaiting his first brief is not a new one and Haldane was writing to his mother on 23 October 1880: 'No briefs yet. One's time is well filled up with reading however . . . . Since coming up one has been getting through between 11 and 12 hours' reading a day and I intend to keep on doing so.' His fee book for 1880 showed that he made only £31 10s. The year 1881 was little better, with a total of £109, and the third year yielded £160. But, as indicated, time did not hang heavily; he read the authorities and text-books copiously when briefs were few, and his old master, William Barber, entrusted him with the preparation of a new edition of Dart's *Vendors and Purchasers*. Haldane, with Barber's assent, associated W. R. Sheldon (a pupil of Haldane's) in the work, which they completed some years later.

Haldane was fond of recounting the curious way in which one of his earliest briefs came to him, and its far-reaching effects. He was shooting in the North of Scotland with a friend whose wife had a large fortune. Among the large party there was a distinguished-looking old gentle-man with gold-rimmed spectacles who, observing that Haldane looked sympathetic, commented on the absence of the champagne to which he was accustomed at dinner. He asked whether Haldane was soon to be in London, and, on his replying that he was, invited him to dine and see the quality not only of his champagne, but of a cellar of claret of which he was very proud. Haldane learned on enquiry that he was one of the principals of a great firm of City solicitors who were watching over the affairs of his hostess. When he got to London he received the invitation he had been promised, and went to dine. There was a party of person-ages eminent in the law whom Haldane was very glad to meet. After dinner they drank some famous Château Margaux of 1864, and then came the *pièce de résistance*—a bottle of still more famous Château Lafite of 1858, then in its perfection. To the dismay of the host, the old gentlemen who were present, and who were in various stages of gout and rheumatism, intimated that it was as much as their lives were worth to drink further, and the host himself by his doctor's orders had been peremptorily cut off. Haldane saw that there was nothing else for it if he wished to save him from real mental pain, so he proceeded to drink out the bottle, paying a well-deserved tribute to the merits of every glass. Presently the others were all stimulated to taste, and the bottle of great wine had a well merited success. Haldane walked home none the worse, and with the feeling that he had done a kindly deed.

Three days later the clerk who shared his garret opened Haldane's door and unexpectedly showed in a young man whom he did not know, carrying a bag. He introduced himself as the son of Haldane's recent host, who, he said, had not ceased to speak not only of the tact of the young barrister who had dined with him but of his genuine appreciation of a great wine. 'With such a one', he said, 'our firm ought to associate itself, for I am certain that his gifts will raise him to the highest eminence in his profession.' The young man then produced from the bag Haldane's first real brief. But he did more; for not only did he send further briefs, but he advised other solicitors in London to come to Haldane, and briefs began to drop in.

Such was Haldane's introduction to the distinguished City solicitors, Freshfields.

Haldane had, in fact, a fine taste in wine and was something of a gourmet. Years later his luncheon and dinner parties at Queen Anne's Gate were to become famous. Even in 1880, when only twenty-four years of age, he was writing to his mother at Cloan telling her that he had '. . . sent down the wine as we arranged, only I sent rather more than we contemplated, as mainly it is *my* friends who drink it up. Two dozen Champagne, two dozen of Sherry, two dozen of Claret . . . I propose that you and I split the bill which amounts to apparently a good deal—£11 9s.'

About this time Haldane made another contact, of even greater moment. His old chief, William Barber, finding that Horace Davey, then the leader of the Chancery Bar, needed a 'devil', recommended Haldane. The great man sent for him and asked him whether he would like to try to read some briefs for him. Haldane jumped at the opportunity, for he realised that to work with Horace Davey was the chance of a lifetime, in spite of the fact that the practice was unremunerative in those days. Some account of this distinguished lawyer is certainly merited, for his influence on Haldane's approach to the law was far-reaching.

Davey was born in 1833, and after a distinguished career at Rugby and University College, Oxford, he was admitted a student of Lincoln's Inn in January 1857, and was called to the Bar in January 1861, having read in John Wickens's chambers, then regarded as the most distinguished school of Equity pleading. From the first, Davey acquired an extensive junior practice in the Chancery courts and when he took silk in 1875 his success as a leader was immediate. It has been said that his legal judgement was intuitive and almost infallible, and his wide acquaintance with foreign law systems gave him a considerable advantage over his competitors, leading to constant employment in the Privy Council and in Scottish cases in the House of Lords. So great became his reputation that at last his 'opinions' came to be regarded as equivalent to judgements and were from time to time accepted as decisions by mutual consent of the parties.

Davey was in politics an advanced Liberal and was for some years in the House of Commons, but he was not a good Parliamentarian. Haldane would recall how Gladstone persuaded Davey to make a speech against the Irish Crimes Bill in the House of Commons. He believed that so great a lawyer would certainly make a decisive contribution to the debate. Davey put aside all his other work and applied himself enthusiastically to the preparation of his speech. Haldane was all along doubtful of Gladstone's choice but was unable when the great day arrived to get to the House of Commons in time to hear Davey. He did, however, meet John Morley a few hours afterwards. 'How did Davey's speech go off?' he asked. 'Go off!' replied Morley; 'it went off exactly like a magnum of soda-water that has stood for two days with the cork out.'

In 1893 Davey was appointed Lord Justice of Appeal in the place of his lifelong friend, Lord Bowen, and in 1894 he succeeded Lord Russell of Killowen as Lord of Appeal in Ordinary, being created a life peer with the title of Lord Davey of Fernhurst. He made a splendid judge, patient and urbane to all who appeared before him (whereas at the Bar he had been admired rather than liked by those who were not admitted to his intimacy), and of unrivalled legal knowledge. His death in 1907 was an almost irreparable loss, both to the House of Lords and to the Judicial Committee of the Privy Council. In private life—with his family and friends—he was a delightful companion and a man of very considerable culture.

Such, briefly, was the man who might be said to have given Richard Haldane his first big chance as an advocate. Haldane's admiration of Davey was unbounded, and in his *Autobiography* he writes:

Davey was, I think, the finest advocate on pure points of law that I have ever seen. In legal matters he had a mind like a razor, and he was accurate to the last degree. It was difficult indeed to put him in a corner, for he knew, almost instinctively, what was a bad point, and avoided all such. He could not cross-examine well, nor could he address a jury. But these were not the things for which he was wanted by the public. It was in the House of Lords and the Judicial Committee of the Privy Council that his power became apparent. Even a great advocate like Charles Russell, although Russell was a fine lawyer, was at a disadvantage against him. Herschell perhaps came nearest, but then Davey knew more than Herschell. I suited him when I had taken enough trouble, for I devoted myself, as he did, to unravelling first principles of law.

The words 'first principles' supply the key to much of Haldane's own character and work. As a barrister he was ill qualified at handling witnesses, nor was he at ease in the rough and tumble of *nisi prius* work, but in the supreme tribunals, where the facts have to be marshalled and brought under principle, Haldane was in his element. He sometimes envied the great advocates their mastery of form in presentation and was conscious that his education had been perhaps too abstract and had not encouraged him to seek knowledge in the world of men and affairs as well as in books. Haldane was more attracted by ideas than by people, and this characteristic developed with the passing of the years. His enjoyment of his friends, who were few, and of his acquaintances, who were many, rested largely on the mental stimulus which they afforded him rather than on their personalities or those more elusive qualities which so often draw people together. This is by no means to suggest that Haldane was devoid of affection, and his kindness was proverbial, but in the main the springs of his life lay in his mind rather than in his heart. Because of this, the 'slings and arrows of outrageous fortune' glanced off the powerful armour of his mind and he was enabled to accept with dignity and courage the blows which were to be aimed at him. This very strength, however, carried within it a certain restriction of character that barred the way to the deeper intimacies of love and friendship, which could have added warmth and life to one so superbly equipped in all else.

The year 1880 saw the return of Gladstone to power with a large majority and Haldane began taking an active interest in politics. He was introduced to Mr Albert Grey (afterwards Earl Grey and Governor-General of Canada) and joined the Albert Grey Committee, which was designed to collect and bring together promising young Liberal speakers. He did a little speaking during the election but his weak voice was a considerable handicap. Writing to his mother in January 1881, he told her that he was going to put himself in the hands of an Italian to have his voice made deeper. 'He says he can improve it', wrote Haldane. Whether or not the Italian had any success we do not know, but it could not have been very great, for Haldane suffered from this disability all his life.

The Albert Grey Committee soon broke up. Haldane and some of his friends felt that Grey's political principles were somewhat vague and erratic. However, they were anxious that the group should not disappear entirely, and, largely through the efforts of Haldane, the Eighty Club was formed (to commemorate the Liberal victory), with Lord Richard Grosvenor as its first President and Haldane as Honorary Secretary. The political scene was full of excitement, largely by reason of the emergence of Parnell. The Land League was active in Ireland and the anxious Chief Secretary (W. E. Forster) was seeking to keep order with the aid of coercion.

To his mother Haldane writes on 22 October 1882:

Last night I dined with the Dalhousies and sat next the Prime Minister. He came late after his great speech but quite unfatigued, and Lady Dalhousie very kindly gave me the opportunity of having a long talk with him, not only during dinner but after dinner in the drawing-room. . . . Mr. Gladstone talked a great deal about Germany as well as about current politics and took a great deal of interest in the conversation as I was the only one of the 9 guests with whom he was not acquainted. I shall not readily forget that evening. . . .

At the time of that memorable evening Gladstone was seventy-three and his young admirer twenty-six.

Whilst, however, life was active and interesting for Haldane, it was by no means without anxiety. Briefs were few and far between, which was depressing enough, but even more so was an attack of rheumatic fever. It was whilst he was still convalescing that he sat at dinner next another briefless barrister a few years older than himself, Herbert Henry Asquith. The two men took to each other at once. Their philosophy of life and political views were, at the time, much the same, and soon an intimate friendship was formed. A few years later they were joined in friendship and political activity by Edward Grey. Henceforward and for many years these three were to work in close association and increasing influence.

Haldane, having recovered from rheumatic fever and seeking further outlets for his tireless energy, became interested in the Working Men's College which had been founded by Frederick Denison Maurice whilst he was a reader at Lincoln's Inn. Maurice had enlisted the help of a number of young barristers as voluntary teachers, and Haldane went there and gave a course of public lectures on 'What is Philosophy?' These were a great success and he followed them by taking a class in philosophy. This was his introduction to what was to become one of the greatest interests of his life, adult education.

About this time he was planning a translation of Schopenhauer's *The World as Will and Idea*. This was a tremendous undertaking and he sought the co-operation of his friend John Kemp, an intimate if shadowy figure in Haldane's life and at one time his 'devil' at Lincoln's Inn. Their association would seem well described in Haldane's own words: 'We conversed much together but the topics were almost exclusively supra-mundane.' The third volume of the translation appeared in 1886; the work had taken four years to complete.

During these early years in London, Haldane became an enthusiastic if infrequent concert-goer and, in particular, a Wagnerite—long before London musical society turned to the great German composer. He enjoyed, too, occasional visits to the theatre, and whilst never a clubman in the accepted sense of the term, he was elected to Brooks's in 1882. With the development of his legal, philosophical, and political work, however, these aesthetic interests ceased to hold him, and his recreation —if such it could be called—took the form of conversation with his friends, and country walks in their company or alone or with his devoted dogs. Whether Haldane was ever an actual member of the famous Sunday Tramps (formed in 1879 by the distinguished man of letters and first editor of *The Dictionary of National Biography*, Sir Leslie Stephen) it is difficult to verify. It is certain, however, that he joined them on many occasions. He was also a prolific letter-writer and one is struck by the variety of subjects discussed both in the letters he wrote and those he received. Letter-writing was still a form of conversation.

The year 1883 witnessed a turn in Haldane's fortunes at the Bar. He had now been associated with Horace Davey for some time, and had not spared himself in service to his chief. Often on Saturdays and Sundays he would work for twelve hours at a stretch. The two men got on well together (and this was something of a triumph for Haldane, as Davey was by no means an easy man), and often Davey would have Haldane in his chambers when there were consultations on cases on which he thought he would like to refer to Haldane, who had previously read them up for Davey. This was valuable experience indeed, but Haldane's appearances in court had been few and of little importance. This situation was suddenly and dramatically changed.

The Scottish Petroleum case, which is fully reported in the Chancery Law Reports for 1883, turned on the question whether a shareholder was entitled to have his name removed from the register of a Company (thereby being relieved from 'calls') on the ground of misrepresentation, he having repudiated informally without taking proceedings in court before the date of a petition upon which an order had been made to wind the Company up. As the Company had gone into liquidation, the case was really a hopeless one, although the authorities were not then in 1883 as precise on the point as they are now. Mr Justice Kay, before whom the application originally came, dismissed it with some contempt. The case was to be heard by the Court of Appeal, and Horace Davey was to lead for the appellant, with Haldane as his Junior. Davey, perhaps not unnaturally, took a hopeless view of the case he was to argue. In the end he proved to be right, but the proof was long delayed. Meanwhile, Haldane studied the brief closely and ransacked the authorities, reporting to Davey on any point of interest or importance. Davey invariably tore to pieces the arguments of his Junior, which was certainly valuable training for what was to come. At length the day arrived for the hearing before the great Sir George Jessel (Master of the Rolls) and two Lord Justices of Appeal. Davey said he had an engagement in another court and in any event he did not think he could argue the case efficiently. This may have been true, but perhaps also he was interested to see how his young colleague would shape 'under fire'. Haldane vividly describes the scene:

Nothing daunted I opened my lips for the first time in the Court of Appeal. Jessel, who caught the point with his unerring quickness, began to play with me in the spirit of a cat with a mouse. But I was so versed, not only in all the learning that had to do with the case, but in a good deal that had not to do with it, that he could not crush me straight off, and presently got intensely interested and combative. No doubt he was quite excited at the vigour with which he was being fought by an unknown

Junior. The result was that the day's argument brought on a relapse of the Bright's disease from which he was suffering. The case had to be adjourned, and in forty-eight hours the Master of the Rolls was dead. He was a very great judge, and my comrades proceeded to reproach me with having killed him.

Thereupon the case had to be re-argued. Davey said he would most certainly not interfere, and left Haldane to reopen the case before Lord Justice Lindley, Lord Justice Fry, and Lord Justice Baggallay. In the fortnight that had elapsed between the two hearings Haldane had so polished his arguments that he succeeded in destroying most of the points on which Mr Justice Kay had relied in deciding against the appellant. At the end of the second day the Court of Appeal, which had grown very interested, called upon the Counsel for the other side, who, not being so well prepared as Haldane in distinguishing the authorities, had a very bad time. When Haldane replied he expressed regret that Davey could not be there to reply in this important case, but such was the impression he had made that Lord Justice Lindley interposed by saying, 'Mr Haldane, the Court of Appeal is of the opinion that your clients have no need to regret the absence of your leader.' Judgement was reserved for many days and at the end, as Davey had predicted, the decision was against Haldane; but his reputation as an advocate was established.

Writing to his mother on 18 April 1883, Haldane says: 'Davey has been much pleased with me. He says he is quite proud of me and that he thinks the argument for the appellants in hopeless case is one of the finest things that has been done at the Chancery Bar for the last year or two.' Two days later Lord Justice Lindley in a letter to Haldane writes, 'Your admirable argument greatly pleased me. . . .' Of such commendation from Bench and Bar a young man of twenty-seven could be justly proud.

Soon after the disposal of the Scottish Petroleum case Haldane had a further opportunity of showing his courage and ability. Davey had been briefed on an application for special leave to appeal by the Government of Quebec. The sum involved was trifling and it seemed doubtful whether the Privy Council would grant leave to appeal against the judgement of the Canadian courts. The matter, however, was of high importance, involving as it did the validity of a statute embodying the Quebec Government policy. Unless the appeal succeeded, the Government of Quebec was likely to fall. The initial problem, however, was to secure the special leave from the Privy Council to appeal, and for this purpose there had to be a preliminary argument to show a *prima facie* case. The Solicitor-General from Quebec had come to London with instructions to obtain the first advocate at the English Bar, and Davey had been selected.

Late in the evening before the case was to be heard, Davey was summoned to continue an argument in a part-heard appeal in the House of Lords—a summons imposing on him a duty which took precedence of that to the Privy Council. No other leader could be found to take so important a brief within a matter of hours of appearance, and in desperation Davey sent his head clerk to Haldane's rooms in Down Street, Piccadilly, to seek his help. Fortunately Haldane was at home and promised to be present at a consultation at the Privy Council arranged for ten o'clock the next morning. Davey hoped that he could persuade the Solicitor-General for Quebec to open the petition himself, but meanwhile Haldane was to read up the case and be prepared if necessary to argue it. Haldane's reaction to so formidable an undertaking can best be described in his own words; they are certainly an indication of his character: 'I was not used to shrinking from responsibility in things which had to be faced, so I told the clerk that it would be all right.' The 'scene' at the Privy Council at ten o'clock next morning had a somewhat high flashpoint!

Davey opened the proceedings by outlining what he considered the mode of presentation. He then informed the Solicitor-General for Quebec that he must open the case himself, as he, Davey, was unfortunately compelled to be in the House of Lords. The agitated and indignant Solicitor-General refused to argue the case himself and stated that his orders quite definitely precluded him from so doing. In any event he certainly did not wish to be the instrument which might bring about the fall of his own Government! At this point young Mr Haldane was introduced, and Davey, having informed the Solicitor-General and Messrs Freshfields (the instructing solicitors) that Haldane knew everything about the case and would open it excellently, took his hat and disappeared into the House of Lords. This was too much for Mr Wiseman, the old Privy Council manager of Freshfields (and later a valued friend of Haldane's), who burst out: 'The house of Freshfield has delivered briefs in their time to Sir Richard Bethel, Sir Hugh Cairns, Sir Roundell Palmer, and other great men, and none of them ever treated the firm as Mr Davey has to-day.' One can have a measure of sympathy with each of the parties concerned, but most of all one is filled with admiration of Haldane, who, at this point, interjected, 'Well, the case will be called in less than five minutes and we had better give up lamentations, and, if you like, I am quite prepared to argue it. I think I know what ought to be said, although, of course, it is a great misfortune that neither the Solicitor-General nor Mr Davey is able to do it himself.' As there was no alternative the Solicitor-General and Mr Wiseman agreed, but with little grace.

Haldane argued the case moderately and well before the Judicial Committee—a considerable ordeal for a young man whose first appearance it was before their Lordships. After much deliberation, Lord Watson (who presided) said that what had been stated satisfied them that leave to appeal should be granted. In spite of this triumph, neither the Solicitor-General for Quebec nor Freshfields said a word of thanks to Haldane; they were still deeply aggrieved at the risk they considered they had been forced to run. However, Freshfields were soon to make amends, and that handsomely. Two or three days later old Mr Wiseman mounted the stairs to Haldane's 'garret' and informed him that the partners of the firm had read the shorthand notes of the brief argument before the Judicial Committee and now wished Haldane to act for them in an important case for the Province of Ontario—this brief marked 150 guineas! Mr Wiseman also said that there might be more briefs to follow, and so indeed it turned out.

Haldane's third year at the Bar brought him in only about £160, but his fourth year (1883–84) yielded about £1,100. He was now being spoken of as an energetic and ingenious Junior, and solicitors were beginning to find their way to 5 New Square in increasing numbers. Haldane thought nothing of working in his chambers until midnight, with a brief interval for dinner at the old Cock Tavern in Fleet Street. The Quebec case 'crisis' was soon forgotten and Davey, who was a consummate leader before the Judicial Committee, was in constant demand. He led Haldane in a number of important cases and almost always to victory. When Davey was appointed a judge (in 1893) Haldane succeeded him in the lead in many constitutional cases, particularly from Canada.

By 1885, with an assured position at the Bar, Haldane felt justified in thinking of entering Parliament. Gladstone's second Administration was drawing to a close. It had been dominated by the Irish question, with the figure of Parnell looming large across the canvas. The story—

complex and tangled—cannot be told in detail here but its main features might briefly be summarised as follows.

Gladstone had assumed office in April 1880 and the Queen's Speech announced that the coercion statute passed by the Conservatives would be allowed to lapse on June 1st. It was hoped to govern Ireland by the ordinary law. Such a policy could succeed only if, at the same time, immediate relief was brought to the Irish tenants. Relief was delayed and the situation deteriorated. Ricks were burned, cattle maimed, dwelling-houses fired, men and women were assaulted, and, finally, life itself, which had previously been spared, was forfeit. On 19 September 1880, Parnell urged that anyone taking a farm from which a tenant had been evicted should be 'isolated from his kind as if he were a leper of old'. The first person to be thus treated was a certain Captain Boycott; his name has added a word to the English language. A terrible and tragic situation had been reached by the autumn of 1880. The agricultural depression, which in 1877 had led to the eviction of 2,177 persons (and 236 agrarian outrages), had by 1880 caused 10,457 evictions (and 2,590 outrages). Parnell's method of 'boycott' soon became an acknowledged weapon. When the Government could stand it no longer, a prosecution for conspiracy was launched (2 November 1880) against the Land League, with Parnell and thirteen others named as defendants. The trial lasted from 13 December 1880 until 25 January 1881, and ended in a disagreement of the jury. This was a triumph for Parnell and the enthusiasm of his followers knew no bounds.

In spite of Cabinet opposition from Gladstone, Chamberlain, and Bright, W. E. Forster (the Chief Secretary for Ireland) introduced his Coercion Bill on 24 January 1881. So great was the obstruction that the Bill did not become law until March 2nd. Its main feature was a suspension of the Habeas Corpus Act. It conferred on the Irish Executive an absolute power of entry and preventive arrest. Gladstone realised, however, that such a measure was doomed to failure unless coupled with some redress of the appalling plight of the Irish tenants. On 7 April 1881 he introduced his second great measure of Irish land reform. It gave the tenants the 'three F.s' (fixity of tenancy, fair rents, and free sale) for which they had been agitating since Butt's day. Its scope and completeness astonished Irish and English Members alike. The historian, Sir Robert Ensor, pertinently remarks, however, 'Its chief flaw was its occasion; as too often in England's dealings with Ireland, the administration conceded to violence and crime what it had denied to reason and justice.' It might be added that not alone in dealings with Ireland is such an attitude adopted.

Parnell saw all this, and the possibility of securing even better terms if he played his cards well. He was able to persuade three-fifths of his followers to abstain from supporting the Bill on Second Reading, while at the same time he took care to save it from being weakened in Committee. Two days after it had been passed by the Commons he deliberately provoked a scene, got himself expelled, and continued to deter the tenants from dropping their agitation and rushing into the Act's new land courts. It was a shrewd move and eventually won better terms from the courts and preserved the support of the Irish-American extremists. The Government, however, were in an impossible position. With the Coercion Act still in force, how could Parnell be left free? At Leeds on October 7th Gladstone declared that the resources of civilisation were not exhausted and six days later Parnell was imprisoned in Kilmainham Jail. This was exactly what Parnell wanted. He wore the halo of martyrdom, but perhaps of even greater importance at that moment was his desire to be out of the way during the confinement of Mrs O'Shea (the wife of Captain O'Shea, an Irish Liberal M.P.), who was expecting a child by Parnell. He was in custody for nearly six months until 1882, and Forster's unsuccessful coercion ran for that period, thus lasting for about a year in all. On April 10th Parnell was permitted leave from prison to visit a married sister whose son was dying in Paris. At Eltham his own daughter (by Mrs O'Shea), born in February 1882, was also dying and Parnell went there on his way to and from Paris. He there saw O'Shea, through whom communications were opened up by Chamberlain and Gladstone. The time was ripe for a settlement, which both sides wanted, but there was one hard obstacle in the way. Some 100,000 Irish tenants owed large arrears of rent and therefore could not take advantage of the Land Act. They all remained liable to eviction. Parnell insisted on a Bill to wipe off the arrears with a contribution from some public source. Chamberlain, a man of great practical genius, saw the need for such a Bill, and it was largely because of his advocacy that a secret informal bargain was struck whereby the Government should introduce an Arrears Bill and Parnell should use his powerful influence to end crime and disorder.

Parnell was released from prison on 2 May 1882. Lord Cowper, the Viceroy, resigned, as also Forster, the Chief Secretary. Their places were taken by Lord Spencer and Lord Frederick Cavendish. Hopes ran high that at last peace would be restored to this tormented country, but tragedy was hiding in the wings. On May 6th, Lord Spencer arrived in Dublin. The same day Lord Frederick Cavendish and Mr Burke, the Under-Secretary, were walking in Phoenix Park within sight and hearing of the Viceregal Lodge, when they were brutally attacked by a band of men who hacked them to death with long surgical knives. Their object was to kill Burke—Cavendish suffered because he was in Burke's company. The assassins belonged to the 'Invincibles', a small murder club that had escaped detection by Dublin Castle, who had been arresting suspects right and left. This brutal murder sent a wave of horror throughout the civilised world. Parnell was deeply distressed and he, John Dillon, and Michael Davitt signed a condemnatory manifesto. Both Gladstone and Parnell were desperately anxious to save the Kilmainham alliance, but the outrage in Phoenix Park made a new and stiffer Crimes Bill inevitable and that drew the opposition of the Parnellites. An Arrears Act was passed (as had been secretly agreed in principle) but not generous enough for most of the tenants to use. Moreover, the 'Invincibles' were still undetected, and murder and outrage continued and increased. Perhaps the most shocking crime in the whole history of agrarian outrages occurred on August 17th, when an entire household at Maamtrasna—father, mother, three sons, and a daughter—were stabbed and battered as they slept, and left for dead. Only one (a small boy) survived his wounds.

The year was drawing to a close, having established a record of murder and attempted murder, when the new Coercion Act bore fruit in the arrest of the 'Invincibles'. Two of them turned Queen's Evidence and in the following April (1883) they were brought to trial. The Phoenix Park conspiracy was exposed and five of those concerned in it were hanged, three sent to penal servitude for life, and one (James Carey, being a councillor of the Dublin Corporation and one of the two who turned Queen's Evidence) was shot dead by an avenger on his way to Natal, whither it was sought to smuggle him. Towards the close of 1883, Irish affairs grew quieter, which suited Parnell alike for personal and political reasons at that time.

In the spring of 1885 rumour had it that Gladstone was preparing a measure for a separate Parliament for Ireland, and the breach between the right wing and the main body of the Liberal Party began to widen. It was not, however, the Irish question which brought about the fall of the Gladstone Administration. The long and tortuous story of our interest in Egypt since the purchase of the Suez Canal shares in 1875 had culminated in our conquest of the country, and the historic appointment in September 1883 of Evelyn Baring (later to become Lord Cromer) as British Agent and Consul-General. He held the post for over twenty-three years.

Two years earlier a native of Dongola—with a none too savoury record as a slave trader and an Egyptian official—had proclaimed himself a Mahdi, or Messiah, and raised a revolt in Kordofan. Misgovernment throughout the area known as the Egyptian Sudan had, since 1880, been atrocious, and the Mahdi's movement spread like wildfire. Egypt was insolvent and disorganised and it would have been wiser to give way, retaining at most Khartoum and the province of Sennaar. The Khedive's Ministers, however, wanted more, and, encouraged by some trivial successes, they decided to send an army under a British officer (Hicks Pasha) to attack the Mahdi in his own country. At this point the British Government made a fatal mistake: they should have vetoed the expedition but instead they did not. Hicks Pasha and his Egyptians were cut to pieces by the Mahdists on 5 November 1883, and Gladstone was faced with a greatly aggravated problem. It was decided to evacuate the whole Sudan south of Wadi Halfa, but how were the many and scattered Egyptian garrisons to be saved? Most pressing were the inland garrisons centred on Khartoum. At length it was decided to send General Charles Gordon, and he left London on 18 January 1884. Baring's assent to this decision had been reluctant. He feared sending Gordon lest his fanatical courage might lead him too far, in which event the British Army might be needed to extricate Gordon himself! Gordon went to Khartoum as Governor-General, with secret instructions to evacuate. Events moved fast and in May 1884 Berler fell to the Mahdists, and Gordon in Khartoum was cut off.

As early as March 26th Baring had urged the Government to make immediate preparations for a military expedition and Wolseley had added his powerful support on April 8th. The British Cabinet, however, allowed matters to drift on until August before reaching a decision. Having lost four precious months, Wolseley was appointed to command an expedition for which little, if any, preparation had been made. He reached Cairo early in September but was not able to start from Wadi Halfa until October 5th. The story of the gallant army which for three months fought its way up the uncharted Nile has been told time and time again. They were within an ace of reaching their objective.

Gordon had sent four steamboats down the Nile and the relieving force made contact with them on the morning of 21 January 1885. Had they gone upstream with reinforcements the same afternoon they would have reached the besieged town on the 25th at the latest. But the start was inexplicably delayed for three days and they did not arrive until the 28th. Gordon's epic defence had ended on January 26th, when the place had been stormed and Gordon killed.

Public indignation—fully shared by the Queen—knew no bounds and was primarily directed at Gladstone. No single event in his career made him more unpopular. It is hard to escape the verdict that the prime cause of the disaster was the Cabinet's inconsequence and neglect of facts. A vote of censure in the Commons was defeated by only fourteen votes. Gladstone's Administration continued until June 1885, when an amendment to the Budget was carried by 264 votes to 252. Gladstone resigned and the Queen sent for Lord Salisbury. Salisbury's minority Government lasted almost exactly seven months.

When Salisbury dissolved Parliament in January 1886, Haldane decided that the time had come for him to seek a seat. He hoped he might become Liberal candidate for West Perthshire, where his home was, but, contrary to expectations, Sir Donald Currie, the sitting Member for the entire county, which had just been divided, chose the western division. Haldane was then invited to contest East Lothian, which for many years had been represented by a member of the Wemyss family. The fight was a hard one but resulted in the ejection of the sitting Member, Lord Elcho, by a large majority. There was great enthusiasm when the news reached Haldane's home. His brother John sent him this account:

Mother asked me to write to you about last night's doings at Cloanden. I suppose she had already told you how the news was received at two yesterday morning. After leaving Cloanden the man who came up with the news seems to have gone to Aberuthven and set the bells ringing. They had apparently just made a bonfire in Auchterarder, mostly with wood taken from the closets in the back-gardens of Auchterarder houses.

Last night there was a bonfire on the hill, a thousand people came up with torches and a band, and there were fireworks afterwards. The people were immensely enthusiastic.

It was at this election that Edward Grey first entered the House of Commons. He too won a long-held Conservative seat (Berwick) for the Liberals. Haldane represented East Lothian unbrokenly for a quarter of a century but had to fight no fewer than eight elections during that time, for it had been by long tradition a Conservative seat. The memory of the Gordon tragedy cost Gladstone a good many votes and his majority over the Conservatives in the new House was only eighty-six, exclusive of the Irish Nationalists. Parnell, however, had swept Catholic Ireland and brought a like number (eighty-six) with him to Westminster. He had achieved what he had been working for during the past five years and became the arbiter in Parliament. He could keep either English Party out of office but only the Liberals were strong enough for him to put them in.

Haldane and a good many more Liberals who were anxious to avoid splitting the Party prematurely thought that Salisbury should have been left in office. However, this was not to be, and after the Government's defeat on an amendment to the Address Gladstone formed his third Administration in February 1886. Lord Herschell, Haldane's connexion by marriage, became Lord Chancellor, and his old chief, Horace Davey, Solicitor-General.

Haldane was now in his thirtieth year—a successful barrister, a Member of Parliament, something of a philosopher, and certainly a man highly regarded in the circles in which he moved. He was conscious of his qualities and of his defects and underrated neither. He realised early in his career at the Bar that he had few of the attributes which go to make the powerful advocate who can sway a jury with his rhetoric, can neutralise a hostile witness, and breathe confidence into a seemingly lost cause. His advocacy was of a different order and was seen at its best when great principles of law were involved, when the search for truth was conducted with quiet dignity before the Privy Council or the House of Lords, rather than in the dramatic and publicised setting of the Old Bailey. This is not to suggest that Haldane had no knowledge of the psychology of advocacy. He realised only too well how necessary it was to secure the sympathy of the tribunal, even when your case in law was a strong one, and to remember the idiosyncrasies of the judges before whom you practised. He was particularly successful in following the movements of mind of the judges as a case proceeded and showing sympathy and understanding without in any way weakening his own arguments. He realised, too, that in the House of Commons he would be wise to confine himself to speaking briefly and to the point on matters on which he had expert knowledge. He was no orator, but his power of lucid exposition was considerable and his sincerity patent.

Gladstone's third Administration had a short life. In it he introduced his Home Rule Bill, which was defeated on Second Reading by thirty votes, ninety-three Liberals (but not Haldane, who was a convinced Home Ruler) voting with the majority. The split in the Liberal ranks was complete and the Liberal Unionists had come into being as a Party.

In the General Election of 1886, Haldane was again returned for East Lothian but with a greatly reduced majority. To his delight his friend Herbert Asquith, whom he had introduced to the Liberals of East Fife, won the seat, and so was initiated a great Parliamentary career. The result of the election was to send back only 191 Liberals to Parliament. Gladstone resigned and Salisbury formed his second Administration. The Liberals were to remain in opposition until 1892. The Conservative Administration saw the eclipse of the brilliant Lord Randolph Churchill, who seemed predestined to be a future Prime Minister, and the emergence of Arthur Balfour, Lord Salisbury's nephew. He had entered Parliament in 1874 as a supporter of Disraeli's last Administration and was appointed Secretary for Scotland by his uncle in his second Government, being given Cabinet rank in November 1886, at the age of thirty-eight.

In the Parliament of 1886 Haldane, Asquith, and Grey drew closely together; they formed the nucleus of a group of Liberals whose prime interest was in social reform. Others who joined them were Arthur Acland (later to become Minister of Education) and Sydney Buxton (later Earl Buxton and Governor-General of the Union of South Africa). Asquith, who had brought a great reputation with him from Oxford, was a splendid speaker and acted as the voice of the group in the House.

The friendship of Haldane, Asquith, and Grey deepened with the passing of the years, for they held similar views on most political subjects and naturally saw much of one another in the House and elsewhere in London when Parliament was sitting. During the recesses there were frequent exchanges of visits between Fallodon, Cloan, and Hampstead. The three men, on the other hand, presented an interesting contrast in character and ability. Haldane with his capacious intellect was, as has already been indicated, more concerned with principles and ideas than with men and things. This was hardly calculated to make him a popular figure in political circles, where principles and ideas are so often sacrificed to more spectacular if less worthy objects. His independence of thought, his subtle powers of persuasion, and his unruffled demeanour ultimately created something of a figure of mystery, which, it must be admitted, Haldane did nothing to destroy. In fact, he rather enjoyed being the 'benevolent conspirator'. His was essentially a modest and gentle character, but with an underlying tenacity of purpose which, together with a splendid intellect, carried him forward in the pursuit of truth as he saw it.

What, then, was the bond of sympathy between Haldane and Grey, apart from agreement on political questions? There is a very revealing passage in Dr G. M. Trevelyan's *Grey of Fallodon* which may well supply the answer. 'Grey, always primarily interested in the perfection of character and personality, was never contented either with himself or others. . . .' Both men were idealists; Haldane perhaps more concerned with the ideal as an idea, whilst Grey looked for its transforming influence in character and personality. In the same passage Dr Trevelyan adds these words: '. . . among public men his own intimate friend, Haldane, ere long came nearest to his ideal'. In 1890 Grey wrote to Haldane in these terms:

Your influence will always be greatly indirect, and it will be your privilege never to be able to measure it. If it were not for you I do not think I should have even the hold on public life which I have now. There are others too more worth influencing. I should say, for instance, that Asquith owed some of the very best of himself to you; in knowing you both I feel as if it was so.

The intimacy of friendship between these two men never wavered and Grey held a unique place in Haldane's affections.

Grey had a most attractive personality and, whilst having little of the intellectual capacity of Haldane or Asquith, was a man of independent mind and advanced views. His character has perhaps been over-sentimentalised in the public mind—the lover of birds and the countryside has been stressed almost to the exclusion of the long years dedicated to the nation's service. Grey, indeed, found the country a source of strength and inspiration, a necessity of his nature; but his entry into public life was a call to service which he could not resist. There were moments when he longed for the quiet country life and to be done with the feverish activity of politics. In such a character this was natural, but his deep instinct for public duty was always strong enough to bring the two sides of his nature into balance.

Edward Grey will constantly reappear in these pages. This, however, is not the moment to pass judgement on his political sagacity or on the momentous years of his Foreign Secretaryship. Suffice it to say at this stage that no man less self-seeking ever entered the political arena and by simplicity and strength of character emerged as one of the central figures in the history of his times.

The third and ultimately the most famous of the trio was Asquith. He was born to succeed. Nature had endowed him with gifts of the highest order: a splendid intellect, a fine presence, faultless diction, and a powerful voice. He was, moreover, ambitious. Haldane and Grey were idealists and so remained to the end. Asquith's character was more complex than that of either of his friends. The superb intellectual equipment which he possessed was in some measure offset by a lack of vision and imagination. When reason, logic, and good sense failed to convince (and no one could more perfectly state a case in these terms), he could not call to his aid that passionate belief which can move men when all else fails. A certain fastidiousness would no doubt have prevented his using such a weapon, even had he possessed it. There was in Asquith an extreme emotional reserve which prevented him from showing the depth of his feelings to any except those nearest and dearest to him. For the rest he was always something of an abstraction, a remote figure. His second marriage in 1894 to the brilliant Margot Tennant carried him into a new world, and gradually the sterner view of life which he and Haldane shared in the early days ceased to attract him. He, like Grey, will play a considerable part in this story and at one point a decisive one, in so far as Haldane was concerned. By any standard Asquith was an outstanding figure in British political history. That is not to say, however, that his character and actions are removed from the realm of controversy. It seems possible that Asquith's great reputation is most likely to suffer by reason of the reluctance of a small body of his admirers to exercise their critical faculties in examining their hero. Pedestals are dangerous contrivances and Asquith can stand very well on his own feet—albeit a little lower than the angels.

Haldane's first speech of any importance was not made until March 1887, when he spoke on the Criminal Law Amendment Bill, Ireland (better known as the Crimes Bill). He deplored the attempt to govern Ireland by coercion, which, he declared, was bound to fail. It was his conviction that Home Rule offered the only statesmanlike solution. Gladstone heard this speech and complimented him on it afterwards. It is typical of Haldane's mind and character that he reached his

conclusions only after profound thought and investigation. In 1886 he
and Asquith had gone to Ireland together and had spent much time
cross-examining both landlords and tenants. They had also been present
at the eviction on the Kenmare estate of the chief local Land Leaguer,
which took place under the protection of seventy police. All they
saw and heard only strengthened their conviction that Home Rule
was the only answer.

It soon became evident that Haldane was a man of independent
judgement, and was by character and outlook something of a political
nonconformist. That is not to suggest that he actively sought to differ
from his Party, but he found it impossible to subscribe to the dictum
'My Party, right or wrong'. With the passing of the years he was
increasingly concerned with the advancement of certain ideas and
ideals in which he believed. What particular Party was the instrument
to bring such changes about was to him of secondary importance. This
detracted in some measure from his Party influence and affiliation.
Ultimately it led him to associate himself with the Labour Party, not, I
would suggest, from purely political motives but because he believed
that the ideals he embraced had the best hope of fulfilment within that
Party. Haldane was often a bad Party politician, but he was a wise and
courageous thinker. The place of such a man in our political life is not
an easy one, but in 1887, at the age of thirty-one, there were few clouds
on the horizon. He was doing well at the Bar in work which he loved,
his political début had been satisfactory, and he enjoyed the companionship of his new friends, Asquith and Grey, and entered enthusiastically
into the plans they formulated for a better world.

About this time, or maybe a little earlier, Haldane had come to know
George Meredith. It may well have been that he was introduced to the
novelist and poet on one of Leslie Stephen's Sunday Tramps when a
call was made on Meredith, then living in his little house at the foot of
Box Hill. The acquaintance ripened into friendship and in later years
Haldane frequently dined with Meredith at Box Hill. Writing to Haldane in 1889, Meredith says:

I am glad that the Côte Rôtie has reached you safely. When sipping it, with a
cogitative brother Scot, do me the favour to count me beside you in soul. Of course
you know the nice conduct of Burgundy. Rhône wines throw an even greater rough-
ness. Therefore they should be stood upright a day before the drinking (lying in a warm
room a day or two); or if this has been forgotten a couple of hours in a kitchen, away
from the fire, will serve your turn.

Haldane found much to delight him in his friendship with Meredith, not least his exquisite hospitality and his splendid conversation. This latter encouraged a Victorian wit to remark, 'By God, George, why don't you write like you talk?'

A far cry from his friendship with Meredith was that with Sidney, and later Beatrice, Webb. There was no rich food or memorable wine at their table but rather, as Professor Tawney so aptly puts it, a 'participation in one of the famous exercises in asceticism described by Mrs Webb as dinners'. There was, however, much stimulating talk and the company was often exciting—Bernard Shaw, Sydney Olivier, Graham Wallas, and others. This remarkable couple believed that evil could be removed by the patient and resolute use of intelligence, science, and goodwill. Exhaustive (and sometimes exhausting) investigation and research were undertaken on innumerable subjects; books, pamphlets, reports, flowed ceaselessly from their pens. Much of it was of great value and their disinterestedness and unselfishness was apparent to all. Haldane was attracted by their earnestness, their encyclopedic knowledge, and their evident desire to 'spread the light' as they saw it. The Webbs (in the early 1900s) formed a small dining club to gather together men of goodwill, irrespective of Party, in an endeavour to put into practice their ideas of a 'welfare State'—and perhaps a new world. This experiment is described by L. S. Amery in the first volume of *My Political Life*:

... the actual form the Brains Trust was to take was a small dining club, to meet at regular intervals for serious discussion and for the subsequent formulation of policy. It was to be called the Coefficients, both to emphasize efficiency as the keynote of the new political grouping, and because policy was to emerge from the contributions of a body of whom each member was supposed to be an expert in his own domain. We were not to be more than a dozen to start with—all contributors, no passengers.

By 8th December the dozen were collected and we made an excellent start, from the gastronomic point of view, by dining with Haldane. Later on our venue shifted to the Ship Tavern in Whitehall and to St. Ermin's Hotel. Our original body consisted of the following: Haldane and Grey, representing law and foreign policy, while active Liberal Imperialism was also represented by H. J. Mackinder, at that time regarded as a coming man in the Party. Sir Clinton Dawkins, recently Finance Member of the Council of India, and a partner in Morgans, represented finance. Professor W. A. S. Hewins, Principal of the London School of Economics, represented economics. Science was represented by Bertrand Russell. Journalism by Leo Maxse, editor of the *National Review*. Sidney Webb stood for knowledge of municipal affairs. W. Pember Reeves, then Agent General for New Zealand, for the colonial point of view. A naval officer and writer, Lieut. Carlyon Bellairs and myself for the fighting services, and H. G. Wells, nominally for literature, really for original thinking on all subjects.

But such concentrated talent found agreement well-nigh impossible to secure, and Amery records:

Anyhow the Coefficients, as a brains trust with a definite political object, petered out almost as soon as they began. But as a dining club for the informal discussion of serious topics they flourished for five or six years. Bertrand Russell dropped out early. But we were joined in the next three years by Sir Henry Birchenough, a business man of wide international experience and chairman of the British South Africa Company, Lord Milner on his return from South Africa, Julian Corbett, the naval historian, J. L. Garvin, Henry Newbolt the poet and, with me the only survivor, John Hugh Smith, now chairman of Hambro's Bank. Later still, in 1907, came Fred Oliver, the biographer of Alexander Hamilton, C. F. G. Masterman, the rising but short-lived Liberal Minister, W. F. Monypenny, former editor of the *Johannesburg Star* and at that time engaged on the life of Disraeli, Repington, *The Times* military critic, E. C. Grenfell (Lord St. Just), Theodore Morison, the Indian educationist, and that erratic but lovable champion of human liberty, Josiah Wedgwood. After that interest began to flag and the club must have faded out in 1908 or 1909.[1]

Haldane never joined the Fabian Society,[2] but he retained his friendship with the Webbs throughout his life. They were to co-operate with him on a number of educational projects near to his heart, and ultimately he and Sidney Webb found themselves as colleagues in the first Labour Government.

Shortly after their election to the House of Commons, Haldane and Asquith began a custom which they continued for several years, that of giving an annual dinner at the Blue Post Inn in Cork Street. To this dinner they invited eight guests, four of them distinguished politicians and the other men eminent in the law or the arts. It was something of a feat that these two young men were able to attract to their table such men as Balfour, Rosebery, Morley, Curzon, Randolph Churchill, James Russell Lowell, and many others.

The early months of 1887 saw the publication in *The Times* of a series of articles on Ireland which contained grave charges against Parnell and the Irish Members in general. On the eve of the Second Reading of the Crimes Bill a letter was published, purporting to be signed by Parnell, in which he implied approval of the Phoenix Park

[1] L. S. Amery, *My Political Life*, Vol. I (Hutchinson).
[2] Haldane remarks in his *Autobiography*, 'I never belonged to the Fabian Society. . . .' Beatrice Webb in her Diary, 12 February 1925, says '. . . Haldane, who by the way has joined the Fabian Society.'!

murders. Parnell declared the letter to be a forgery and demanded that the facts be investigated by a Select Committee. The Government actually appointed a Statutory Commission (of three judges) to examine not only the authenticity of the letter, but also the charges made in *The Times*. The proceedings dragged on until 1889. Parnell was represented by the brilliant Sir Charles Russell (later to become Lord Russell of Killowen), with Asquith as his Junior. The end was dramatic. A man named Pigott who had produced the letter in *The Times* broke down under cross-examination, confessed to forgery, and committed suicide. *The Times* was called upon to pay the whole cost of the enquiry, which amounted to £250,000. It had already paid £30,000 in acquiring the material for its articles, which it is only fair to say had been bought in good faith.

The Eighty Club celebrated this event by a dinner, with Lord Rosebery in the chair. Parnell came as Sir Charles Russell's guest, and Haldane sat next the Irish leader. The Pigott letter having been proved a forgery, Parnell appeared to regard the whole incident as beneath his notice and did not refer to it during dinner nor in his speech after dinner.

Queen Victoria celebrated her first Jubilee in 1887. Unfortunately, the bitter feelings aroused by the Irish question and a good deal of unemployment somewhat marred the general rejoicings. In November there were angry meetings in Trafalgar Square and some rioting. The police thereupon prohibited further meetings in the Square on the ground that it was Crown property. This had the opposite effect to what they hoped and a huge demonstration was organised in defence of the rights of free speech and free meetings. Cunninghame Graham and John Burns addressed the crowd and were both arrested on the charge of incitement to disturbance. Haldane had come to know Cunninghame Graham well during visits to South and East London, and whilst thinking that his friend had behaved foolishly, he at once left a case on which he was engaged and stood bail for him. The two men were tried at the Central Criminal Court, Asquith appearing in defence and Haldane giving evidence on their behalf. In cross-examination an attempt was made to make him commit himself to approval of incitement to violence. This Haldane found no difficulty in combating, but in spite of his evidence and Asquith's advocacy the two men were sent to prison for six weeks.

It was about this time or a little earlier that Haldane, through a letter he wrote to *The Times* in criticism of Chamberlain, came to know John Morley. In his *Autobiography* Haldane says of Morley, 'I think his was the most interesting personality I ever knew.' Morley, who was born in 1838, spent his early years as a free-lance journalist—a hard struggle indeed until he secured more permanent work with *The Saturday Review*. One of his Saturday essays arrested the attention of John Stuart Mill and brought Morley into personal contact and lasting friendship with the great teacher and philosopher of Liberalism, described by Gladstone as the 'Saint of Rationalism'. Morley later became editor of *The Fortnightly Review*, a position which he held for fifteen years. In his hands the *Fortnightly* soon became a national organ of Liberal opinion and much of the best work published came from Morley's own pen. He made two unsuccessful attempts to enter Parliament, at Blackburn in 1867 and at Westminster in 1880. His Parliamentary ambition was at last gratified by his election early in 1883 for Newcastle-upon-Tyne. Morley was a complex character—a man of deep learning, an outstanding biographer, and a forceful and penetrating critic. He was moreover an idealist who sought to be a man of affairs, and an agnostic with a sense of piety and of the mystery of life and death not always to be found among the orthodox. Morley might well have achieved even greater eminence and influence than he did had he devoted himself to literature and political criticism. He was, however, ambitious to become an outstanding political figure, for which he was unsuited by his nature, physical as well as mental. He early came under the dominating influence of Gladstone, which, whilst it helped him to write a brilliant study of a great man, may have been damaging to his originality. Throughout his life he was impressed (sometimes over-impressed) by powerful personalities, particularly if they expressed themselves in men of action. It was the man of affairs, the soldier, the diplomatist, or the ruler who moved Morley most. Perhaps he saw in them qualities which he admired but did not possess. Notwithstanding the fact that his political aspirations were never fully realised, Morley played an important part in the life of his country for many years. He remained constant to the faith which he had reasoned out in early manhood, and this consistency of thought and conduct gave moral weight to his opinion and helped to raise the standards of public life. It is not difficult to appreciate the attraction Morley had for Haldane. Here was a radical with a highly critical mind, a man to whom the Party meant less than the faith it represented, an agnostic with a deep sense of piety, and withal a fine scholar and stimulating conversationalist. Their friendship lasted until Morley's death in 1923.

Towards the end of 1887 Haldane applied to the Lord Chancellor for a silk gown and was naturally disappointed when nothing came of it. Lord Macnaghten (a very great judge and a man of enduring charm and humour), to whom Haldane had sent a copy of Dart's *Vendors and Purchasers*, wrote to him:

Seriously I am sorry that the Lord Chancellor has not seen fit to comply with your application, that is, if you are disappointed. For your own good I think it better you should wait a little, it is a disadvantage, especially if you are thinking of 'special' work, to be too young. What the grounds of the Lord Chancellor's action were I don't know. Youth or Cunninghame Graham or both combined.

Some twenty-five years later, Haldane (as Lord Chancellor) was to find Macnaghten as a colleague on the Bench and so benefit from his vast experience—he had been a judge for a quarter of a century.

About this time, 1888, the little group of young Members which included Haldane and his friends Asquith and Grey began to expand. Dinners were held sometimes at the National Liberal Club and sometimes at the Savoy, to which politicians outside the group were invited. Rosebery and Morley frequently attended, as also Frank Lockwood, who afterwards became Solicitor-General. Lockwood's premature death in 1897 in what seemed the full tide of his inexhaustible vitality was a great loss to his countless friends. A natural actor, a most gifted caricaturist and highly successful barrister and Member of Parliament, there was no more popular figure either at the Bar or in the House of Commons.

Gladstone was still the venerated figure to whom the group continued to look for inspiration, but the daily work of leadership was in the hands of Sir William Harcourt. Harcourt was one of the greatest of the old school of Parliamentarians. He was an indefatigable worker and his speeches were monuments of closely reasoned arguments. He was a tremendous fighter and was never happier or heard to better advantage than when the battle was a hopeless one against overwhelming odds. An aristocrat, he was impatient of mediocrity, but beneath a somewhat aggressive manner was a deep kindliness of spirit which endeared him to those who knew him well. He preserved his friendships intact through the vicissitudes of a long and distinguished Parliamentary career.

Harcourt was somewhat critical of Haldane and his friends. They did not, in his view, give enough time to Parliament and were too interested and involved in outside affairs. Haldane in particular was always a somewhat unknown quantity from a Party point of view, and one can at least have some understanding of Harcourt's irritation as virtual leader of the Party. He would naturally have liked to harness the outstanding ability of Haldane and his friends to the Party machine. Haldane, on the other hand, apart from his deep interest in educational and social questions, was finding his work at the Bar as a prominent Junior more and more exacting. This, in part at least, accounted for increasingly intermittent appearances and speeches in the House. At the same time he found himself out of sympathy with the radical wing of the Party, which he thought had an undue influence on the Liberal policy, and he was anxious that his group of political friends should make their weight more felt. To this end he sought to secure the leadership of Lord Rosebery. Writing to his friend Ronald Ferguson (later Lord Novar) in November 1889, he describes a visit to Mentmore.

The plot thickens! After arranging everything as well as I could with John Morley and Asquith I went to Mentmore on Saturday. There I found Henry Fowler, to whom John Morley had spoken. I had a quiet talk with Rosebery in his dressing room. On Sunday we gave a mixed crew of guests, consisting of Christopher Sykes, Sandhurst, Smalley, Oscar Browning, and Canon MacColl, the slip and went out for a walk in the rain with Fowler. Rosebery has been thinking over the plan almost continuously since it was broached to him, and he and Fowler began by cross-examining me closely as to what you, Asquith, Edward Grey and I proposed. I said we aimed not at a new party—still less at a conspiracy—but simply at the formation of a group bound together by a common point of view, rather than any definite organisation. This group should aim at gaining the confidence of the public by its constructive propositions, and should be the means of gaining a position from which to criticise with the utmost frankness and firmness the people with whose ideas we were at present being associated, i.e. Labouchere and Company. We would at the same time be perfectly loyal to our front bench while stimulating it to give the party a lead.

Rosebery said that it had occurred to him that a meeting of the party might be summoned by Mr. G. to strengthen his leadership. I pointed out that however useful this might be Laby & Co. would surely profess loyalty and then ask what Mr. G. proposed in home affairs. The answer would be that neither Mr. G. nor anyone else had an idea to broach. Our function would be to prevent Laby & Co. stepping in to fill the gap by applying ourselves to a constructive programme. Rosebery on reflection concurred in this, and finally he and Fowler agreed very warmly with our proposal. We are—this is the result—to look to John Morley and Fowler on the Front bench as those with whom we are informally, but in substance, in touch and we are to distribute amongst ourselves the work of thinking and working out an effective programme. This is provided that the proposal is ratified, as I think it will be, at a dinner which John Morley is to convene on the 13th at which Fowler, Asquith, Sydney Buxton, Grey and I are to be present. Everything is being kept quiet at present, Harcourt being rather the *bête noire* of the gathering. Rosebery made many very acute suggestions. He is really keen about the whole business, and will, I think, give us most astute guidance and help. Of course we are only at the beginning of wisdom but we must buckle to and put our backs into the business; our credit is at stake.

I had, as far as I am concerned, much the most satisfactory two days with Rosebery I ever had. I know that you always wanted to promote a friendship between us and he has always been kindly to me. But there have been differences in point of view, which the dour Northumbrian nature, I have inherited from my mother, would never, hitherto, permit me to minimise. But on this occasion all this has been merged in common interests and I find myself at one with him on his Imperial policy. He is going in a few days to advocate a programme of regular Colonial Conferences and to this even a Morleyite like myself can wish God speed!

What we have to do at home is to try to gain the confidence of the electors and to mould their opinions. To my dying day, I think, I shall maintain the proposition, based on the analogy of my own mind, that a democracy has not got, as is assumed in practice, a body of definite opinion, for the expression of which in Parliament it seeks delegates, but that it is an assembly of human beings earnestly seeking guidance from those of whose sympathies it is sure.

Haldane was in his element in conducting such negotiations. A degree of secrecy appealed to his nature. The opening words of his letter, 'The plot thickens!', indicate his almost boyish delight in the task, although he is at pains to point out that a 'conspiracy' was in no way intended. It was perhaps this air of mystery so enjoyed by Haldane that helped towards the deep misunderstanding of his work and character which developed with the passing years.

The Morley dinner was duly held and the proposal endorsed, thereby bringing the Liberal Imperialist group into being, Haldane undertaking as his particular share of the group's work the extension of university education, women's suffrage, and housing. It also saw the beginning of a considerable political intimacy between Haldane and Rosebery, although Rosebery's active leadership of the group was never fully realised. This was in part due to the paralysing blow he suffered in November 1890 by the death of his wife. Rosebery had relied greatly on her wisdom and serenity of character, and it is doubtful if he ever wholly recovered from this blow. For the next eighteen months he withdrew entirely from politics and it was only under great pressure from Gladstone and a strongly worded letter from the Prince of Wales indicating the wishes of the Queen that he was persuaded to join Gladstone's fourth and last Administration as Foreign Secretary in 1892.

Rosebery was one of the most enigmatic figures of his time. Destined, it seemed, to rank as one of the greatest political figures of his day, he failed to fulfil the outstanding promise of his early years. In spite of his great distinction there were in his character qualities which militated against his success as a Party leader. He was deeply sensitive to criticism, and fear of failure in any enterprise made him easily discouraged. Succeeding to his title as a minor, he had served no apprenticeship in the House of Commons, and even those of his own Party in the Lower House never understood him, least of all the dominant Nonconformists. This handsome, rich, eloquent, horse-racing aristocrat was little to their liking. Rosebery, who had served in Gladstone's third and fourth Cabinets as Foreign Secretary, succeeded to the Premiership in March 1894. His Administration lasted little over a year and he never assumed office again. He ceased to be associated with National Liberalism in 1905 and thereafter was less and less active in politics. He died in 1929.

In bringing this chapter to a close, mention should be made of two friendships which brought Haldane much happiness and a great deal of intellectual stimulus. Peter Hume Brown had come to Cloan as tutor to the younger Haldane children and soon gained their affection, which was to continue until his death in 1918. At one time he occupied the Chair of Ancient History in the University of Edinburgh and he gradually established his reputation as a historian. The personality and teaching of Goethe had early attracted Haldane and he found in Hume Brown a kindred spirit. The two men began to spend each Easter recess in Germany, assembling material for a Life of Goethe which Hume Brown was then projecting. These visits meant a great deal to both men and Haldane records:

We used at first to make our headquarters at Weimar. Afterwards we chose Ilmenau as our centre for inquiry. But we visited Jena, Eisenach, Wetzlar, and Göttingen for the purposes of our search for materials. I have always regretted that Hume Brown's reticent disposition prevented him from using the notes we made about places in which Goethe delighted but of which there is little record even in the voluminous Lives of him which have been written. There was, for instance, Schloss Dornburg on the Saale, a place described at page 646 of Hume Brown's book, where Goethe used to take Frau von Stein and her children to stay. We found there a very old custodian, not indeed old enough to have known Goethe, but who had learned from his father, who had been custodian before him, in Goethe's time, something of the way in which Goethe lived when there. He remained, so our informant told us, shut up daily with his work in his room, and was not accessible until four in the afternoon excepting to Frau von Stein, who went in and out as she pleased to talk to the great man. The latter used to come into the garden in the afternoon and to cut out profiles in black paper of her and the children. Examples of these, some of which had been preserved, the old custodian showed us. Then at Ilmenau there was not only the Kickelhahn, which Goethe, when at Ilmenau, used to ascend regularly, but the old seat by the summer-house on the top, on which he sat while composing the famous lyric, transcribed by him in pencil on its wall, 'Ueber allen Gipfeln ist Ruh'. I have sat with my companion scores of times on that old seat, and with him have watched the summits fading in the oncoming evening as the poem describes them. We tracked out, too, the walks Goethe took with the Grand Duke, and rested by the favourite waterfall described in his poems.

Weimar itself, although now modernised, remained the same so far as the park which Goethe laid out and the banks of the Ilm were concerned. The old librarian of the Schloss showed us the small room which Goethe selected for his work in prefer-ence to the larger one. Why? 'Because,' said the old man, 'from its window he could look at the windows of the Frau von Stein.'

After one of their typical fortnights at Ilmenau, Hume Brown wrote to Haldane:

Before taking up my burden I must write a line to say how greatly I have enjoyed this our last visit to cherished Ilmenau. It seems as if each successive visit were pleasanter than the last. I cannot but feel that it is to you that I owe this annual refreshment for mind and body, for though Ilmenau has many attractions, it is seeing it with you that makes it what it is in my memory and imagination. I never have such talks as we have at the Tanne (the Inn) and in the glades of the Thüringer Wald, and it is to these I look forward rather than to the beauties of the Kickelhahn. What I feel is that these our annual pilgrimages have given a zest to these last years which nothing else has given. To-day I feel somewhat indisposed to take up my wonted tasks, but I pull myself together when I remember that Ilmenau is in vain if it does not enable me to go more briskly through the rest of the year. Still it is not in human nature not to feel the contrast *here* and *there*.[1]

Preliminary studies on the *Youth of Goethe* appeared in 1913, but Hume Brown died before the *Life* was wholly complete and by his desire Haldane and his sister finished the work and arranged for its publication. Haldane found the finished scholarship of Hume Brown much to his liking, as also his insatiable curiosity and unbounded toler-ance. Nothing delighted Hume Brown more in conversation than to abandon the precision of his scholarship and talk of subjects on which his mind was not yet made up, hazard conjectures, argue moot points, and allow the quick and genial scepticism of his nature full play. Haldane found in Hume Brown a most welcome relief from the intense political life which claimed him more and more with the passage of time. They made many journeys to Germany together, even

[1] *Richard Burdon Haldane: an Autobiography* (Hodder & Stoughton).

during the time that Haldane was War Minister, and Hume Brown's death in 1918 was a loss he felt most deeply. Haldane was a man of few intimate friends and Hume Brown was one of them.

In 1888 appeared *Robert Elsmere* by Mrs Humphry Ward. It was an immediate success, and Haldane, deeply interested in the writer's understanding of the philosophy of religion, sought and made her acquaintance. Mrs Humphry Ward believed that Christianity could be revitalised by discarding its miraculous element and emphasising its social mission. She gave practical evidence of this belief in the great work she did for recreational centres for London children and for the education of crippled children. Her practical achievements were no less notable than her literary success. Such an outlook greatly attracted Haldane and before long a warm friendship developed which was to continue until Mrs Humphry Ward's death in 1920.

As his work and interests developed, the ties with home, and particularly with his mother, showed no signs of lessening. There was a constant exchange of letters, and whenever he could make the journey to Cloan he did so, even if, as sometimes happened, it meant only a few hours at home. As time passed, Haldane entertained increasingly at Cloan. He was a splendid host and was never happier than when he could combine the delights of family life with the company of his friends.

It will be remembered that soon after Haldane was elected to Parliament in 1885 the Liberals went into opposition, Lord Salisbury forming in 1886 his second Administration, which was to continue until 1892. Algernon Cecil (a kindly but discerning critic) commenting on his uncle's election address in 1853 says that it 'exhibited the readiness to abide by the *fait accompli* (in this case the abolition of the Corn Laws) which was one of his more salient characteristics'. Salisbury was a right-wing Conservative, critical and unsanguine of temperament, and sceptical of the value of popular reforms. His deepest concerns were the defence of property, religious education, and foreign affairs. His distrust of democracy was not a distrust of the poorer classes as such (they were no better nor worse than other men), but a fear (and not without foundation) that power could easily become divorced from responsibility, that sheer weight of numbers might overwhelm and destroy the political system which had been so laboriously evolved over the centuries. That the system was imperfect he would be the first to admit, but it could only be satisfactorily changed by a gradual process.

Such views inclined him (and his Party) to a defence of the *status quo*. With democracy gathering speed at what sometimes appeared an alarming rate, Lord Salisbury's high-minded scepticism was not without value. When great changes are under way it is well for the country that there are men whose critical temper remains intact. Above all else Salisbury was a great patriot. He had none of the popular appeal of Gladstone and Disraeli, but his massive wisdom and calm temper were dedicated to the service of his country.

CHAPTER 4

The Widening Horizon: 1890–1895

The sun shone for Richard Haldane in the early days of 1890. He had applied to the Lord Chancellor for silk in the autumn of 1889 and this time his application was granted and he was called within the Bar in January 1890. He was in his thirty-fourth year and had just completed ten years as a barrister. On the eve of the presentation of his patent he wrote to his mother:

It is certainly a step. I am supposed to be the youngest Q.C. made for fifty years. It is clear that I am going to get a chance. I hear already of briefs coming to me. Soares [his clerk] is nearly off his head with excitement and pomposity as he has to arrange the ceremonies tomorrow. When we have been sworn in and the Lord Chancellor has delivered our patents to us, we are to go round all the Courts where we are formally called in in each to plead. We are attired in full court dress and the procession is a very tedious one. My youth as a Q.C. is the subject of much gossip in the press and about legal circles and is an advertisement in itself. A silk gown seems to be regarded as something very wonderful by the public. Perhaps from familiarity with its wearers I do not possess so much reverence for it. Anyhow it is quite curious to see what social importance even people like Lady Rosebery and the Spencers attach to it. I think it must be the lace ruffles, which, by the way, I have declined to wear.

The Lord Chancellor (Lord Halsbury), before whom Haldane had often appeared, in handing him his patent whispered 'I think this will be a great success.'

In March he became engaged to Miss Valentine Munro Ferguson, whom he had known for some years, and his happiness seemed complete. They had many tastes in common and much the same outlook on life—or so it appeared. Towards the end of April, Haldane had left her to return to his work after a visit they had made together in Devonshire. Suddenly, without previous warning, she broke off the engagement, saying she felt she had misunderstood herself. Her family, who were intimate friends of Haldane, and some of her friends hoped that she might reconsider her decision, but this was not to be; it was irrevocable.

What brought about this seemingly sudden reversion of feeling it is hard to conjecture. It has been suggested that Miss Ferguson found herself unable to face the somewhat rarefied intellectual atmosphere of the life which she would be called upon to live had she married Haldane. Or, again, that Haldane had few of the personal attributes likely to attract a young woman. These are plausible if seemingly somewhat inadequate explanations of Miss Ferguson's sudden change of heart. Haldane himself, in writing to his mother at the time, suggests 'some sudden breakdown of feeling which was due simply to some physical cause. There was, if I am right, a mental aberration.' Miss Ferguson died unmarried seven years later and there is not lacking evidence to support Haldane's explanation.

Whatever the reason may have been, the blow to Haldane was almost overwhelming. He went abroad for some weeks in an endeavour to find relief. Gradually the clouds lifted and he accepted with touching dignity and rare generosity of spirit the shattering of his hopes. To an aunt in the autumn of the following year he wrote:

I never ceased to care for her and I never judged her nor blamed her. She was always the same to me, and her memory will be with me through all my days—just as she was when in the last days of March seven years ago she and I came to Banbury Road.

Old feelings surge up now, feelings which I had suppressed but could not destroy.

And towards the end of his life in his *Autobiography* he wrote:

To this hour I treasure the memory of these five happy weeks, and bless her name for the return she made in them to my devotion to her, and for the feeling inspired apparently in both of us. I came to realise afterwards, when the pain was past, that my love for her, though it failed, had brought to me not loss but great gain. For it enlarged the meaning and content of life for me. All is now over. She died in 1897, but the memory of her is a precious possession.

Haldane never married, but one is tempted to speculate as to the effect a happy marriage would have had on his character and work. Perhaps his interest in people as such would have been enlarged. Perhaps the 'man of mystery' would have receded and he would have been better understood by his fellow countrymen. His personal life would almost certainly have been enlarged and enriched in countless ways. But this was not to be. He found a measure of compensation in his work, which absorbed him increasingly and, as the years passed, developed in interest and importance. Haldane's devotion to his family and particularly to his mother became, with the shattering of his hopes, the focal point of his affections, and may have helped to preclude—

unconsciously, to be sure—the chance of his forming any other attachment which might have led to marriage. His somewhat limited emotional life appears to have derived from two sources: a memory of happiness tasted but unfulfilled, and a deep attachment to his mother.

In the summer of 1890, Haldane and his brother John went to Germany, combining a holiday with the opportunity of renewing contacts with German philosophers. A letter which he wrote from Freiburg to Mrs Humphry Ward serves to indicate his outlook at that time.

You were concerned about me when I left and it has always been a pleasure to write and talk to you, so I do so now. I came here last week with my brother—partly for a holiday, and partly to do some work. There are several people in the University here whom we wanted to see, and we wished particularly to do what we could towards working out the next step in getting hold of a subject, on which we wrote a little book[1] together several years ago, and at which we have in our different ways been busy ever since—the relation of the organic world, in which life and God and psychical phenomena are the distinguishing conceptions, to the sphere of pure mechanism. Prof. Weissmann is the chief apostle of the reduction of the former to the latter, and we are spending a good deal of time with him. It is really the same problem as the one in which you are so much engrossed, that of the possibility of lifting up Christianity from the region of *Vorstellung* into that of *Begriff*. Weissmann is analogous to those who would make the whole truth depend on an historical 'yes' or 'no'. So it is, too, with Hegelianism. We have long since thrown over the cast-iron deduction of the Universe which Hegel presented to us. Yet the real point of view is there, and I, for one, who owe nearly everything of the little I know to him, cannot listen with patience to ignorant sneers at his memory. God will remain the supreme reality to us, though 'we sweep the heavens with our glass and find Him not', and so, too, there is a life which is greater than that on earth, though we may not be able to figure to ourselves a personal continuance after death. Kant taught the world that Nature as we know it could not be adequately represented in relations and categories of time and space, and Hegel carried this still further. To what extent then have philosophy and biology not inflicted loss on themselves and distorted these very facts, by mere dogmatic assumption that the relations of life are reducible and must be so to those of mechanism? This is what my brother's book will seek to answer from the point of view of a biologist who has read his Kant and Hegel, and striven to escape from dogmatism, and it is the philosophical chapters I am working at with him.

So I have begun this letter with a whole screed of philosophy. I do not apologise for it, for I know how much this point of view has meant to yourself in other regions. It seems to pervade everything. Even politics have become for me penetrated with it. It helps us like reading St. Paul—in examining the meaning of Socialism—and in asking whether the self-conserving power of a living organism can be expressed adequately or at all in terms of the doctrines of physicists.

I am also writing a short review of Schopenhauer's *Aphorisms* and reading *The Ring and the Book*. What a power genius has of grasping and expressing situations and

[1] *Essays in Philosophical Criticism* (Longmans, Green & Co. Ltd.)

the career of one who, in the opinion of the historian, Sir Robert Ensor, ranks next in stature to the four supreme Parliamentarians of Queen Victoria's reign, Peel, Palmerston, Disraeli, and Gladstone.

The death of Parnell, followed by deep dissension among his followers, brought relief to the Conservative Party but little prospect of the Liberals' securing an overwhelming Home Rule majority at the next General Election. For Haldane this meant that, with an election drawing near, he had to devote more time to his constituency and to his political work generally. This he welcomed and he rarely refused an invitation to speak, although this entailed, more often than not, travelling with a bag of briefs to study on his journeys.

In the summer of 1891, Haldane suffered a great loss in the death of Mrs Asquith, a woman of singularly lovely character. She was much more to him than the wife of his great friend Asquith. To Haldane, after her death, Asquith wrote: 'There are none of my friends for whom she had a more real affection or whose fortunes—bright or clouded—she followed with a more vivid or loving interest.'

This same summer was to bring him happier tidings in the engagement of his friend Sidney Webb to Beatrice Potter. Writing to Haldane on 25 July 1891, Webb said:

. . . Of course I am awfully happy: but I feel all the responsibility, both that I should not spoil a life which I regard as of high value to the world; and that I, too, should not fail to give the fullest possible product in return for my own happiness. Therefore I am teutonically grave about it; not anxious, but trying to realise *how much* is demanded. 'On the Ethical Responsibilities of the Exceptionally Lucky' is an unwritten chapter in Ethics which I am inclined to ponder.

However, I know I can't possibly earn it all, any more than I have deserved it all—so that all I can do is to do my utmost to make the combination as potent for good as possible. . . .

This unique partnership was to last for over fifty years.

Salisbury dissolved Parliament in June 1892. The resulting General Election was scarcely a triumph for the Liberals. Gladstone's majority in Midlothian fell to 700—previously it had been numbered in thousands. Haldane and Asquith were both returned, but with greatly reduced majorities. The Conservative Government were, however, defeated by 40 votes on the Address, the Irish Party going into the lobby with the Liberals. Salisbury thereupon resigned and the Queen sent for Gladstone, who formed his fourth and last Administration; he was then eighty-two years of age.

Whilst Gladstone was forming his Ministry, Haldane wrote a letter to Sir Algernon West, Gladstone's Chief Whip, which is indicative not only of Haldane's far-sightedness but of a generosity of outlook which is refreshing in the political field:

My desire in writing now, if I may do so without seeming to intrude, is to emphasise the importance of a step towards securing the confidence of the nascent body of opinion in the constituencies which cares little for any Irish policy and concentrates itself on social questions. As I said to you, I am convinced that the man in our ranks who possesses, beyond anyone else of his standing, the confidence of the labour party, using the term in its widest sense, is Arthur Acland. He has, as none of us younger men has, the personal respect of not only prominent leaders like Tom Mann and Burns, but of the great body of artisans of the northern and midland counties. He is looked on by them, and I think rightly, as having done more really good work in the House of Commons in the last five sessions than any other member of his standing. Besides this he is regarded by the Welsh members as one of themselves, because of the services he has rendered them in intermediate education and other matters. I believe that I am expressing the sentiments of the bulk of the rank and file in the House when I say that it will be a deep disappointment if he is not placed in a position under Mr. Gladstone where he may exercise real influence and attract to us still more of that confidence of the industrial classes on which we greatly depend to-day for our future. What occurs to me I venture to suggest for consideration in the light of your experience. Why should not the opportunity be taken of doing what would at once be useful and popular, making the labour department of the Board of Trade a reality by putting it under his charge and extending its functions? The Secretary of the Board of Trade is not a very important office at present. Might not a vice-presidency be created, with the announcement that the labour department was to be extended and annexed to it, and Acland be made the first vice-president? This may be a difficult step. I have not the knowledge to judge, but I am satisfied that both generally and in connection with Acland it would be very popular. The minister in charge of the labour department would have abundance to do and Acland's large experience in settling industrial disputes and getting at the minds of the working people would enable him to develop the functions of his office from the very first. He is in an unique position. Burt, for example, is regarded with an approach to hostility by the Labour Party, and there is probably no man within their ranks whom their jealousies would permit to fill the most prominent position in the Labour sphere, witness the defeat of Tom Mann by Burns and others for the secretaryship of the Amalgamated Engineers. But in Acland there is no sense of rivalry. They look on him as a highly educated outsider who has devoted his life to the study of the relations of capital and labour. I am aware that to talk of a Labour ministry is to suggest what is easy to speak of and difficult to do, but if some step towards it could now be taken I feel sure that it would strengthen Mr. Gladstone's position both in the Constituencies and in the present House of Commons.

A Ministry of Labour did not mature for another thirty years but a place was found for Acland at the Board of Education. He retired from